SCOTTISH
INTERNATIONAL
FOOTBALL
MISCELLANY

BRIAN BELTON
FOREWORD BY PAT NEVIN

First published in hardback 2007
by Pennant Books

Text copyright © Brian Belton 2007

The moral right of the author has been asserted.

British Library Cataloguing-in-Publication Data:
A catalogue record for this book is available from
The British Library

ISBN 978-1-906015-06-0

Design & Typeset by Envy Design Ltd

Printed and bound in Great Britain by CPI Group (UK) Ltd

Pictures reproduced with kind permission of PA Photos

SFA logo reproduced by kind permission of SFA

The views, opinions and comments expressed or made in this publication are those of the author or otherwise and in no way represent the views and opinions of the Scottish Football Association.

Every reasonable effort has been made to acknowledge the ownership of copyright material included in this book. Any errors that have inadvertently occurred will be corrected in subsequent editions provided notification is sent to the publisher.

Pennant Books
A division of Pennant Publishing Ltd
PO Box 5675
London W1A 3FB
www.pennantbooks.com

— FOREWORD —

The Scottish International Football Miscellany is irreverent and informative, funny and factual. It is the perfect entertaining book to read prior to going down the pub and bewildering your pals with your intricate knowledge of the international side and some of its many foibles.

Stories of events we all know, or at least think we do, are retold in the 'Caledonian Chronicles'; however, they are sometimes from unusual sources and, as such, give different perspectives than we may be used to.

Random potted biographies of international players young and old vie for space with researched lists that can double as a useful encyclopaedia.

Tartan Army aficionados will fondly recognise many of the anecdotes but even they might be surprised at some of the quotes that have been resurrected having being buried for many years.

It is hard to top Bill Shankly's one-liner when informed that he was getting a golden boot for services to the game and they needed to know his size: 'If it is gold, tell them I take a size 28.' It underlines the type and speed of humour that we Scots are famous for, which is evident throughout the book.

There are also enough classic malapropisms included to make all of us who are pundits in the game blush with embarrassment – sorry, 'get a pure dead riddie', to use the correct West of Scotland terminology.

It is, however, the candid self-observations, many of which are included here, that sum us up best when it comes to the national sport. Whenever walking out for an international game where Ally McCoist was involved, we would always hear him shout the same thing in the tunnel: 'Mon Scotland'.

They were the precise words, but more importantly said in exactly the same accent, of the majority of the fans waiting outside. They were a call to remind us all that we were fans too, except we just happened to be lucky enough to be getting a game that day. Two little words, but they reminded us that it was unacceptable to do anything less than equal the passion coming down from the stands right from the start.

It is the passion for the game that sets us apart and that passion is at the root of the entertainment in this book, but maybe it also sets us apart from reality at times, as Hugh Dallas recalls here, 'I refereed Croatia against

Bosnia at a time when they were at war with each other and it was an easier game to handle than the Old Firm.'

Maybe it is time we learned to love the game, to enjoy it for what it is, celebrate the differences between Celtic and Rangers or Scotland and England. Here is another quote ... 'Aye Right!'

Pat Nevin – Scottish International

— INTRODUCTION —

Hampden Park, November 1984, 9.20pm. A 33-year-old man has given his all. For more than 30 minutes, he has run, toiled and tried every means his considerable football intellect has put at his disposal to make himself a target for his team-mates who, like him, wear the lion rampant over their hearts. Although seemingly at the very limit of his energy reserves and beginning to look ready to make way for a substitute, from somewhere deep in his soul, he summons up the power to sprint towards the corner flag at the end of the right flank.

A throw-in sends the ball beyond his left side. In a single motion, he twists and attacks his opponent's goal. His arms are hanging low and his long flaxen hair is shaking like a lion's mane as he picks up the well-measured square pass. The most capped player in the history of his nation takes control of the ball gracefully; he passes a Spanish defender to float into the penalty area; on a path made of guile and skill he reaches that crucial angle, the point at which he knows no moment would give a more opportune strike. He strokes the ball with the inside of his left foot; and it spirals on its logical course inside the left-hand post. Once more, Dalglish has scored a classically Scottish goal for Scotland.

Every Scottish football supporter will have a goal like that in their minds, one that will stay with them forever. It will be made differently, it will have its own distinctive character, but, no matter how unique, it will have Scotland written right through it. It might be Joe Jordan's crashing header that defeated the Czechs or John Greig's effort against Italy in the dying seconds of the game. But these great flashes in time are but tips of the great berg that are the chronicles of the passion of Caledonia that is built on an ephemera of facts and fables, ranging from sea-sickness in the late 19th century sailing to Belfast to meet the best of the Irish to a hundred years later dealing with problems with cabin-pressure flying to face continental opposition.

When the fervour of the tartan nation has met its equivalent in Europe or South America, blood has been mixed with the sweat and tears, but Scottish football is never far from emotional and political storms. For instance, in 1892, when a goal was awarded to Scotland after Jimmy Ellis put a drive through a hole in the net, the furious Irish spectators almost put their threats concerning the rigging and the referee into practice. Following the first international soccer match in world history in 1872, the initial clashes between England and Scotland showed a distinctly northern dominance. The boys in blue tasted just a single defeat in 31 internationals between March 1873 and March 1888 and, for the first time since the 1707 Act of Union, Scottish nationalism had found a mass means to express itself and Scotland found a realm in which it was possible to dominate the dominators. Things would never be the same again!

William McGregor, a Scotsman, was one of the prime movers in organising the world's first football league in England. Born in Braco, Perthshire, he had been introduced to football in the first part of the 1850s by stonemasons working at Earl Cairns's residence in Duneira. After playing in what time they had off, they left the ball to boys like William when they went back to work.

Other Scotsmen like Johnny Madden and Jacky Robertson took the game around the world. They were the midwives to the sport in places as far apart as Czechoslovakia, Uruguay and Hungary. John Dick (formerly of Airdrie) coached in Prague and John Cameron (who had played for Queen's Park and Scotland) in Dresden. Cameron was interned by the Germans in the First World War.

Back in the mid-1800s the lad who was able to kick the ball highest was held in esteem, but soon Scottish football developed its own qualities. According to the former manager of the Scottish national team Andy Roxburgh, 'We Scots endure a harsh, changeable climate ... We display toughness and adaptability in everyday life, and in the way we play soccer. Due to historical influences, Scottish football is often passionate, adventurous, creative and open, yet tempered to a degree with functional rigidity and discipline.'

If there is such a thing as a 'Scottish way' of playing football it is probably not systemic in any manner, but more of an informal type of organisational attitude based on individual expression and freedom, premised on an ethic that says something like, 'If you are unable to pass your opponent, pass the ball'. This credo has produced a tradition of exciting games and skilful players. At the end of the 1920s, a period when Scottish football was dominant, exponents like Alan Morton, Hughie Gallacher and Alec Jackson, three of the 'Wembley Wizards', were held in the same regard as Maradona, Pele and Cruyff would be in the future.

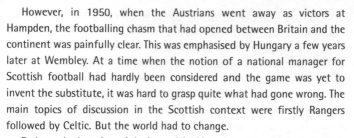

However, in 1950, when the Austrians went away as victors at Hampden, the footballing chasm that had opened between Britain and the continent was painfully clear. This was emphasised by Hungary a few years later at Wembley. At a time when the notion of a national manager for Scottish football had hardly been considered and the game was yet to invent the substitute, it was hard to grasp quite what had gone wrong. The main topics of discussion in the Scottish context were firstly Rangers followed by Celtic. But the world had to change.

Perhaps the last sign of the inward-looking character of British football came in 1984 when the British Championship was abandoned as a largely irrelevant exercise. By that time Scottish football support was more widespread than at any time in the past. Players were chosen from a wider selection of clubs, and the Scottish identity was almost as much to the fore in World Cup matches as it had been when facing the 'Auld Enemy'. At that point, measuring achievement by the number of games played in World Cup Finals (a detrimental standard to Scotland), bearing in mind near-misses on goal-difference and the rebuttal of the chance to compete in Rio in 1950, Scotland were sixth in the world ratings of success relative to population size. The list read: Uruguay, Northern Ireland, Sweden, Austria, Hungary and Scotland. This was a relatively golden period for Scottish football, but it was based on a tradition of zeal, self-belief and sheer will to punch above the collective national weight. For a comparatively diminutive country, Scotland has colossal football proficiency, and the population enthusiastically await almost any international game.

In the 1978 World Cup Finals, following Scotland's 1–1 draw with Iran, it was claimed that the game had coincided with a 25 per cent rise in absenteeism in Glasgow schools. At the same time economists were involved in research into the effect the game had on industrial output. According to Kenny Dalglish, playing for Scotland is 'all about pride and passion ... It's an experience which never fails to make you feel proud to be a Scot'.

Now, as we move towards the end of the first decade of the 21st century, more than a thousand Scotsmen have worn the navy-blue shirts, emblazoned with the red lion soul of their nation. They have fought with fire in their hearts against the odds, engulfed by the sound of the Hampden Park hordes. This is the background against which the *Scotland Miscellany* has been written. It is not a history or an encyclopaedia, but a

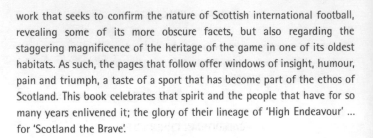

work that seeks to confirm the nature of Scottish international football, revealing some of its more obscure facets, but also regarding the staggering magnificence of the heritage of the game in one of its oldest habitats. As such, the pages that follow offer windows of insight, humour, pain and triumph, a taste of a sport that has become part of the ethos of Scotland. This book celebrates that spirit and the people that have for so many years enlivened it; the glory of their lineage of 'High Endeavour' ... for 'Scotland the Brave'.

— AUTHOR'S NOTE —

The material called upon in this book has been taken from books and newspapers. Where possible, I have consulted newspapers from other countries, but my lack of languages (like Icelandic, Farsi and Serbo-Croatian) was, at times, a drawback.

Statistics come from a number of sources. Official records are not always complete so newspapers were consulted to help compile teams, captains, goalscorers, attendances and referees. The spelling of referees' names may not always be reliable. Attendances ending in three zeros should be treated warily, and there are usually discrepancies between 'tickets sold' and 'attendances on the day'.

On some occasions, newspapers differed in who they accredited as the Scotland captain. Sometimes a skipper was appointed when the team was selected but later withdrew through injury or for any number of reasons lost to the researcher – these include Davie Meiklejohn (v Ireland in 1931), Andy Cunningham (v Ireland in 1924) and Jimmy Simpson (v Czechoslovakia in 1937).

Other interesting if frustrating dilemmas also present themselves over the great history of Scottish football, early goalscorers (before 1909) are one such challenge. So, if statistics on goalscorers differ from others you may come across, please note that I have 'awarded' the goals to those players most commonly cited as scoring or who are said to have scored by the most reliable sources.

All statistics are up to 7 September 2007.

— SGIAN DUBH QUOTE —

Today's top players only want to play in London or for Manchester United. That's what happened when I tried to sign Alan Shearer and he went to Blackburn.

Graeme Souness (54 caps)

— CALEDONIAN CHRONICLES —

The Sportsman newspaper of 5 February 1870 published a letter from the Honorary Secretary of the English Football Association, Mr Charles W. Alcock. It announced that a football match would be played in London, 'between the leading representatives of the Scotch and English sections'. This would be the first soccer game between England and Scotland. The teams met on 5 March at Kennington Oval. The Scottish side which met England was:

J. Kirkpatrick (Civil Service, captain)   G.G. Kennedy (Wanderers)
A.F. Kinnaird (Old Etonians)   W. Lindsay (Old Wykehamists)
R.E. Crawford (Harrow)   W.A. Hamilton (Old Harrovians)
H.W. Primrose (Civil Service)   G.F. Congreve (Old Rugbeians)
C.E. Nepean (Oxford University)   R. Smith (Queen's Park)
Quintin Hogg (Wanderers)

The game finished as a 1–1 draw.

That first match was contested at a time when rugby and association rules overlapped. For example, during the first seven-and-a-half years of Queen's Park's existence, the club never conceded a single goal, but the scoring system at that time included goals *and* touchdowns; on 29 May 1869, Queen's Park beat Hamilton Gymnasium by four goals and nine touchdowns. Two brothers, James and Robert Smith, who played for Queen's Park at that time, had a big influence on the development of international football.

The enthusiasm and enterprise of James Smith was demonstrated by one of his touchdowns against Hamilton Gymnasium; he ripped through a hedge into the next field to get to the ball first, tearing his clothing as well as bruising and scratching most of his body.

SCOTTISH RESULTS IN THE 21ST CENTURY

(note: Scottish goals are noted first – e.g. 2–0 represents a Scottish win)

Game No.	Date	Venue	Opponent	Score	Competition
605	29.03.2000	Glasgow	France	0–2	
606	26.04.2000	Arnhem	Netherlands	0–0	
607	30.05.2000	Dublin	Rep. of Ireland	2–1	
608	02.09.2000	Riga	Latvia	1–0	WCq
609	07.10.2000	San Marino	San Marino	2–0	WCq
610	11.10.2000	Zagreb	Croatia	1–1	WCq
611	15.11.2000	Glasgow	Australia	0–2	
612	24.03.2001	Glasgow	Belgium	2–2	WCq
613	28.03.2001	Glasgow	San Marino	4–0	WCq
614	25.04.2001	Bydgoszcz	Poland	1–1	
615	01.09.2001	Glasgow	Croatia	0–0	WCq
616	05.09.2001	Brussels	Belgium	0–2	WCq
617	06.10.2001	Glasgow	Latvia	2–1	WCq
618	27.03.2002	Paris	France	0–5	
619	17.04.2002	Pittodrie	Nigeria	1–2	
620	16.05.2002	Busan	South Korea	1–4	
621	20.05.2002	Hong Kong	South Africa	0–2	
622	21.08.2002	Glasgow	Denmark	0–1	
623	07.09.2002	Toftir	Faroe Islands	2–2	ECq
624	12.10.2002	Reykjavik	Iceland	2–0	ECq
625	15.10.2002	Easter Road	Canada	3–1	
626	20.11.2002	Braga	Portugal	0–2	
627	12.02.2003	Glasgow	Rep. of Ireland	0–2	
628	29.03.2003	Glasgow	Iceland	2–1	ECq
629	02.04.2003	Kaunas	Lithuania	0–1	ECq
630	30.04.2003	Glasgow	Austria	0–2	
631	27.05.2003	Edinburgh	New Zealand	1–1	
632	07.06.2003	Glasgow	Germany	1–1	ECq
633	20.08.2003	Oslo	Norway	0–0	
634	06.09.2003	Glasgow	Faroe Islands	3–1	ECq
635	10.09.2003	Dortmund	Germany	1–2	ECq
636	11.10.2003	Glasgow	Lithuania	1–0	ECq

637	15.11.2003	Glasgow	Holland	1–0	ECq
638	19.11.2003	Amsterdam	Holland	0–6	ECq
639	18.02.2004	Cardiff	Wales	0–4	
640	31.03.2004	Glasgow	Romania	1–2	
641	28.04.2004	Copenhagen	Denmark	0–1	
642	27.05.2004	Tallinn	Estonia	1–0	
643	30.05.2004	Edinburgh	Trin. & Tobago	4–1	
644	18.08.2004	Glasgow	Hungary	0–3	
645	03.09.2004	Valencia	Spain	1–1	
646	08.09.2004	Glasgow	Slovenia	0–0	WCq
647	09.10.2004	Glasgow	Norway	0–1	WCq
648	13.10.2004	Chisinau	Moldova	1–1	WCq
649	17.11.2004	Edinburgh	Sweden	1–4	
650	26.03.2005	Milan	Italy	0–2	WCq
651	04.06.2005	Glasgow	Moldova	2–0	WCq
652	08.06.2005	Minsk	Belarus	0–0	WCq
653	17.08.2005	Graz	Austria	2–2	
654	03.09.2005	Glasgow	Italy	1–1	WCq
655	07.09.2005	Oslo	Norway	2–1	WCq
656	08.10.2005	Glasgow	Belarus	0–1	WCq
657	12.10.2005	Celje	Slovenia	3–0	WCq
658	12.11.2005	Glasgow	United States	1–1	
659	01.03.2006	Glasgow	Switzerland	1–3	
660	11.05.2006	Kobe	Bulgaria	5–1	
661	13.05.2006	Saitama	Japan	0–0	
662	02.09.2006	Glasgow	Faroe Islands	6–0	ECq
663	06.09.2006	Kaunas	Lithuania	2–1	ECq
664	07.10.2006	Glasgow	France	1–0	ECq
665	11.10.2006	Kiev	Ukraine	0–2	ECq
666	24.03.2007	Glasgow	Georgia	2–1	ECq
667	28.03.2007	Bari	Italy	0–2	ECq
668	30.05.2007	Vienna	Austria	1–0	
669	06.06.2007	Toftir	Faroe Islands	2–0	ECq
670	22.08.2007	Aberdeen	South Afica	1–0	

Played 66 Won 24 Lost 25 Drawn 17
Thanks to Jostein Nygård for the above information.

Scottish Internationals born this day – 1 January
Angus Douglas (1889); John Crum (1912)

Scottish Internationals born this day – 2 January
Hugh Long (1923); Andrew (Andy) Paton (1923);
James Anton (Jim) Blyth (1953); Scot Gemmill (1971)

— SGIAN DUBH QUOTE —

*On my first day as Scotland manager I had to call off practice
after half an hour, because nobody could get the ball off wee
Jimmy Johnstone.*

Tommy Docherty (25 caps and former Scotland manager)

Scottish Internationals born this day – 3 January
James Marshall (1908); David Duff (Davie) Holt (1936)

Scottish International born this day – 4 January
Alan McLaren (1971)

— SGIAN DUBH QUOTE —

*They get to about 30 yards out and then everything goes square
and a bit pedantic.*

Charlie Nicholas (20 caps)

Scottish International born this day – 5 January
Joseph Taylor (1851)

— SALTIRE SEMINAR —

The first set of brothers to appear in an international team were Harold and
Moses McNeil, who played for Scotland against Wales on 25 March 1876.

Scottish Internationals born this day – 6 January
George Anderson (1877); James Alfred (Jimmy) Blair (1918);
James John Stewart (Stewart) Imlach (1932);
William McInanny (Willie) Carr (1950)

— A WEE JOKE —

A nurse at Glasgow General Infirmary told an industrial tribunal how she tried to stop the fight between two top doctors which resulted in one of them being sacked by the hospital.

'I pulled them apart', said Alice Magee, 32, who could see Dr Cage was in tears. 'I asked him what it was about and he sobbed, "It's that man on E ward, you know, the one with the England pyjamas. Dr Harper has just told him that he's only got two weeks left to live."

'I told him there was nothing more we could do for him and he had to be told.

'Dr Cage said, "I know that, but I wanted to tell the bastard."'

Scottish Internationals born this day – 7 January
John Robertson Auld (1862); George Clark Phillips Brown (1907)

Scottish International born this day – 8 January
Edward John (Ted) MacDougall (1947)

— SALTIRE SEMINAR —

The FIFA code for Scotland is SCO.

Scottish Internationals born this day – 9 January
Isaac (Ike) Clarke (1915); Bryan Lovell Dalton (1917);
Stephen (Steve) Crawford (1974)

— BERSERKER BIOG - NEIL ALEXANDER —

Born in Edinburgh on 10 March 1978, Neil made an early impact as a goalkeeper, making his debut for the National Under-21 side while still a teenager at his first professional club, Stenhousemuir. Alexander was two seasons with Ochilview then moved to Livingston. After three years, in the summer of 2001, he joined Cardiff City. Neil notched up 10 Under-21 caps, and was a regular reserve goalkeeper for Scotland before making his senior debut as a second-half substitute in March 2006 in the home defeat by Switzerland. He currently has three senior caps.

Scottish Internationals born this day – 10 January
William Allan Lambie (1873); James Young (1882);
William Beveridge (Billy) Liddell (1922); David (Davie) Wilson (1939)

— SGIAN DUBH QUOTE —

The fans like to see him wear his shirt on his sleeve.

Kenny Dalglish (102 caps)

Scottish Internationals born this day – 11 January
James (Jimmy) Scoular (1925);
Joseph (Joe) Montgomery Harper (1948)

— CALEDONIAN CHRONICLES —

The first international game created enough interest for the organiser C.W. Alcock to write another letter the following November, this time to the *Glasgow Herald*. The missive asked for Scotsmen to assist in staging a second game on 19 November, when once more the Oval would host the meeting.

When Alcock made his second challenge, in November 1870, Robert Smith, who had moved to South Norwood, England, was nominated by Queen's Park to organise the Scotland team because he was based in London. He pulled together a London-based team that included MP W.H. Gladstone (the son of the then Prime Minister) who had been obliged to pull out of the first match 'owing to the exigencies of his political duties'.

Quintin Hogg, philanthropist and grandfather of Mrs Thatcher's Lord Chancellor, was another Scottish player as were A.K. Smith and Will Lindsay, who later played *against* Scotland for England in official internationals.

The Scots were defeated 1–0 in the second international. There were three more such matches before the first official international was played.

Although these games were to be designated as 'unofficial' because the rules were not precisely defined and selection was unrepresentative, they do have historical and social importance.

Scottish International born this day – 12 January
Peter Andrews (1852)

— SGIAN DUBH QUOTE —

Football games turn on things that are done by players.

Willie Miller (65 caps)

Scottish International born this day – 13 January
Bernard (Barney) Battles (1875)

— SCOTLAND'S WOMEN —

Anna Signeul – National Coach

In March 2005, Anna Signeul joined the Scottish Football Association, replacing Vera Pauw, who after four years had led Scotland's women to a position where they were respected throughout Europe.

Signeul played 240 matches in Damallsvenskan, Sweden's premier division, for more than two decades. She was player/coach for IK Brage, Stomsbro If and Tyreso FF. In 1996, Anna became head coach of the youth programme in Sweden, and guided the Swedes to victory in the UEFA Under-18 Championship in 1999. Anna is respected throughout football and has compiled technical reports for FIFA as an observer at major championships such as the UEFA Women's Championship Finals. Her target for the Scottish side is to consolidate the nation's position within Europe's best 20 female national teams.

CURRENT SQUAD (7 SEPTEMBER 2007)

Name	Club	D.O.B	Position	Caps	Goals	Debut
Anderson, Holly	Fulham	31.12.84	Defender	0	0	
Barr, Michelle	Vermont Lady Voltage	19.10.78	Defender	87	1	v Rep of Ireland 1996
Brolly, Denise	Florida Atlantic University	19.11.80	Midfielder	6	0	v Italy March 2006
Brown, Linda	FC Kilmarnock	25.09.68	Forward	48	20	v Rep of Ireland 1983
Bruce, Alana	Forfar Farmington	22.05.82	Forward	8	2	v Belarus Sept 2000
Burns, Amanda	Hibernian LFC	25.05.77	Forward	57	2	v Rep of Ireland 2001
Cook, Stacey	Hibernian LFC	09.11.80	Defender	60	10	v Moldova April 2000
Crichton, Leanne	Edinburgh LFC	06.06.87	Midfield	1	0	v Belgium September 2006
Dieke, Ifeoma	Qbik	25.02.81	Defender	28	0	v Greece 2004
Fay, Gemma	Hibernian LFC	09.12.81	Goalkeeper	80	0	v Czech Republic May 1998
Ferguson, Julie	Hibernian LFC	10.02.79	Midfield	19	0	v England 2003
Fleeting, Julie	Arsenal LFC	18.12.80	Forward	96	98	v Wales Nov 1996
Gilmour, Mhairi	Hibernian LFC	09.06.80	Forward	39	2	v Brazil 1996
Grant, Nicky	Hamilton Academical LFC	13.08.76	Midfield	95	7	v Italy 1993
Grant, Suzanne	Hibernian LFC	17.04.84	Forward	42	3	v Northern Ireland Nov 2000
Grant, Shelley	Glasgow City LFC	17.04.84	Defender	1	0	v England April 2005
Hamill, Pauline	Hibernian LFC	18.12.71	Forward	100	17	v England April 1992
James, Donna	Glasgow City LFC	26.01.84	Forward	37	5	v France March 2000
Johnstone, Claire	Thor Akureyri FC	11.01.82	Goalkeeper	20	0	v Moldova April 1999
Jones, Rhonda	Florida Atlantic University	30.03.79	Defender	49	2	v Estonia 1999
Kerr, Shelley	Hibernian LFC	15.10.69	Defender	45	2	v England April 1989
Lappin, Suzanne	Glasgow City LFC	13.10.86	Midfield	2	0	v Finland August 2006

Liddell, Pamela	Hamilton Academical LFC	11.06.86	Forward	8	0	v Russia August 2005
Little, Kim	Hibernian LFC	29.06.90	Midfield	7	0	v Japan February 2007
Love, Joanne	Celtic LFC	06.12.85	Midfield	58	2	v Canada March 2002
Malone, Suzanne	Hamilton Academical LFC	04.10.84	Forward	25	3	v Belgium May 2003
McBride, Kirsty	Hibernian LFC	09.09.85	Midfield	31	0	v Portugal 2003
McCandlish, Jenna	Hibernian LFC	22.05.80	Goalkeeper	0	0	
McDonald, Amy	Queen's Park LFC	17.10.85	Defender	13	0	v Italy 2006
McFarlane, Jane	Hibernian LFC	11.04.78	Forward	3	0	v China March 2003
McWhinnie, Debbie	Hibernian LFC	31.01.81	Forward	45	10	v Wales March 2002
Murray, Joelle	Hibernian LFC	07.11.86	Defender	1	0	
Pearson, Marlene	Hibernian LFC	12.05.79	Forward	3	0	v Australia 2003
Ralph, Julia	Aberdeen LFC	27.11.82	Forward	14	3	v Holland Sept 2000
Robertson, Suzanne	Hibernian LFC	03.07.75	Defender	11	0	v Wales Oct 2001
Ross, Leanne	Glasgow City LFC	08.07.81	Defender	14	0	v Switzerland April 2006
Smith, Julie	FC Kilmarnock	03.10.73	Defender	73	0	v Spain Sept 1998
Sneddon, Megan	Glasgow City LFC	09.09.85	Midfield	41	2	v USA Sept 2002
Sommerville, Jayne	Glasgow City LFC	20.09.86	Defender	10	0	v Northern Ireland July 2005
Thomson, Hollie	Hamilton Academical LFC	25.12.86	Midfield	3	0	v Russia May 2006

Scotland Captain – Julie Fleeting, Arsenal & Scotland

With 95 goals, Fleeting is her country's most prolific female goalscorer. She is also the first Scottish player to turn out in the WUSA professional league in the USA. Making her debut v Wales, Julie broke into the Scottish side at the age of 15. Now 26 years old, she has 95 international caps.

Julie, a qualified teacher, joined Arsenal after two extremely successful seasons with San Diego Spirit where she was elected 'Most Valuable Player' by her team-mates and coaches and had the honour of winning her club's 'Golden Boot'.

A consistent scorer with the Gunners in the English Premier League, Fleeting was part of the Arsenal side that won the FA Women's Cup against Leeds United in 2006, scoring one of the five goals that defeated the Peacocks.

At the 7th Annual FA Women's Football Awards in June 2005, Julie was voted 'Players' Player of the Year'.

Scottish Internationals born this day – 14 January
David Wilson (1884); John (Jocky) Scott (1948)

— SGIAN DUBH QUOTE —

Walter Smith has come down from the directors' box to tinkle with his tactical formation.

Jock Brown (Commentator, STV and Setanta)

Scottish International born this day – 15 January
Robert Middleton (1903)

Scottish Internationals born this day – 16 January
Robert Glen (1875); John (Jock) Govan (1923);
James (Jimmy) Watson (1924); Alexander James (Alex) Cropley (1951);
Derek Riordan (1983); Craig Beattie (1984)

— BARRY RAMMY – ON THE MARCH WITH ALLY'S ARMY —

Scotland invaded Liverpool on 12 October 1977 for the World Cup qualifying group 7 (second leg) match against Wales and the volume of their supporters at Anfield (most of the 50,850 present) blocked out the contribution of the Royal Welsh Fusiliers band. The Welsh resistance was determined but it was not enough to halt the Scottish march to the World Cup Finals, fired up by Ally MacLeod's prediction that his team were capable of winning the trophy.

The Welsh FA had given up ground advantage because Ninian Park's 10,000-attendance limit under the government's newly introduced safety regulations was not viable.

Scotland needed a win to make sure of their place in the World Cup Finals but had a worrying injury list, including Bruce Rioch and Danny McGrain, although Wales, who required at least a draw to keep their hopes alive, were also missing a few first choices, most significantly Leighton James and Ian Evans, who had broken a leg 10 days earlier. But the Scots had last lost to Wales in 1964 and were firm favourites.

This was Ally MacLeod's ninth game as Scotland manager and his side might have scored twice in the frenzied first 20 minutes of the game. One journalist of the time made the rather odd analogy: 'players chased the ball like 20 pairs of hands seeking a bar of soap in a bath'.

Wales resisted the initial onslaught and took control for a time midway through the first half.

A minute after the whistle blew to start the second half, Willie Donachie was booked, which meant he missed the first match of the World Cup Finals.

As the clock approached the 60-minute mark, John Toshack broke for Wales, but Alan Rough managed to get a touch to his shot and send it on to the bar. Eight minutes after this, Dai Davies made a brilliant save that started a goalmouth melee, but Scotland were unable to get the ball across the Welsh goal line

With just 11 minutes of the match remaining, a long Willie Johnston throw-in led to Joe Jordan and Dave Jones vying to get to the ball first; a hand touched the ball and the referee pointed to the spot. The Welsh protest was vigorous and protracted, but Don Masson, after what seemed like forever, stepped up to cannon the ball to the right of Davies as the keeper leaped the wrong way.

The remonstrations continue to this day, most neutrals seeing that Jordan had had a crucial 'hand' in Scotland's victory.

Three minutes from time, Scotland guaranteed their trip to Argentina with a spectacular goal. Martin Buchan, an 82nd-minute substitute for Sandy Jardine, crossed the ball to the head of Kenny Dalglish, who marked his 50th cap (only the fourth player to have achieved the magic half-century at that time) with a goal.

The full-time whistle signalled the start of some wild scenes of Scottish joy, but the police advised MacLeod not to take his team on a lap of honour for safety reasons.

Wales manager: Mike Smith
Scotland manager: Ally MacLeod
Referee: Robert Wurtz (France)

SCOTLAND	CAPS	CLUB	GOALS	WALES
Alan Rough	16	Partick Thistle		William David Davies
Sandy Jardine (Buchan, 82)	32	Rangers		Roderick John Thomas
Willie Donachie	27	Manchester City		Joseph Patrick Jones
Don Masson (Captain)	14	Queens Park Rangers	79 P	John Francis Mahoney
Gordon McQueen	17	Leeds United		David Edward Jones
Tom Forsyth	16	Rangers		Leighton Phillips
Kenny Dalglish	50	Liverpool	87	Brian Flynn
Asa Hartford	21	Manchester City		Peter Anthony Sayer
Joe Jordan	27	Leeds United		Terence Charles Yorath
Lou Macari	21	Manchester United		John Benjamin Toshack
Willie Johnston	19	West Bromwich Albion		Michael Reginald Thomas
Martin Buchan (Jardine, 82)	27	Manchester United		

Scottish Internationals born this day – 17 January
Albert Thoroughgood Buick (1875);
John Gillespie (Jackie) Henderson (1932); Edwin (Eddie) Gray (1948)

— SGIAN DUBH QUOTE —

If we'd won, it would have meant an historic double-treble. But we weren't even thinking about that.

Walter Smith (former Scotland manager)

Scottish Internationals born this day – 18 January
Peter Russell Weir (1958); Peter Canero (1981)

— A WEE JOKE —

An England fan is trapped on a remote desert island with a sheep and a dog. Soon, the sheep starts looking really attractive to the England fan. However, whenever he approaches the sheep, the dog growls in a threatening manner.

The England fan takes the dog to the opposite side of the island, giving it some food as a distraction. He runs back to the sheep only to find the dog there growling at him. The England fan ties the dog to a tree with a large leash. He goes back to the sheep only to find the dog again growling with a gnawed-off leash around its neck.

By now, the England fan is getting depressed and frustrated. As he sits under a palm tree staring out to sea, a beautiful woman in a tight-fitting wet suit emerges from the surf.

She asks him who he is and, taking pity upon his lonely state, asks if there's ANYTHING she could do for him. The England fan thinks for a moment and then responds, 'Could you take the dog for a walk?'

Scottish Internationals born this day – 19 January
John Gillespie (1872); Robert (Bobby) Moncur (1945)

— CALEDONIAN CHRONICLES – THE FIRST BRITISH CHAMPIONSHIP? —

In 1872, Queen's Park were keen to try their strength against Wanderers, at that point acknowledged as England's strongest side. The Scots suggested a 'semi-international' wherein Queen's Park would call exclusively on Scottish players, and Wanderers would field only Englishmen.

But when Queen's Park were drawn against Wanderers in the last four of the English Cup the idea got shelved. Both clubs sent out their strongest sides to fight out a 0–0 draw in London. Queen's Park could not finance the trip south to contest the replay and pulled out of the competition.

It was then that C.W. Alcock suggested that the London-Scots v London-English should be replaced with a proper Scotland v England fixture to be played alternately in Glasgow and London, back-to-back with the rugby international fixture that had just been inaugurated.

SCOTLAND IN THE 1990s

Game No.	Date	Venue	Opponent	Score	Competition
513	28.03.1990	Glasgow	Argentina	1–0	
514	25.04.1990	Glasgow	East Germany	0–1	
515	16.05.1990	Aberdeen	Egypt	1–3	
516	19.05.1990	Glasgow	Poland	1–1	
517	28.05.1990	Valletta	Malta	2–1	
518	11.06.1990	Genoa	Costa Rica	0–1	
519	16.06.1990	Genoa	Sweden	2–1	WC
520	20.06.1990	Turin	Brazil	0–1	WC
521	12.09.1990	Glasgow	Romania	2–1	ECq
522	17.10.1990	Glasgow	Switzerland	2–1	ECq
523	14.11.1990	Sofia	Bulgaria	1–1	ECq
524	06.02.1991	Glasgow	Soviet Union	0–1	
525	27.03.1991	Glasgow	Bulgaria	1–1	ECq
526	01.05.1991	Serravalle	San Marino	2–0	ECq
527	11.09.1991	Berne	Switzerland	2–2	ECq
528	16.10.1991	Bucharest	Romania	0–1	ECq
529	13.11.1991	Glasgow	San Marino	4–0	ECq
530	19.02.1992	Glasgow	Northern Ireland	1–0	
531	25.03.1992	Glasgow	Finland	1–1	
532	17.05.1992	Denver	United States	1–0	
533	21.05.1992	Toronto	Canada	3–1	
534	03.06.1992	Oslo	Norway	0–0	
535	12.06.1992	Gothenburg	Netherlands	0–1	EC
536	15.06.1992	Norrköping	Germany	0–2	EC
537	18.06.1992	Norrköping	CIS	3–0	EC
538	09.09.1992	Berne	Switzerland	1–3	WCq
539	14.10.1992	Glasgow	Portugal	0–0	WCq
540	18.11.1992	Glasgow	Italy	0–0	WCq
541	17.02.1993	Glasgow	Malta	3–0	WCq
542	24.03.1993	Glasgow	Germany	0–1	
543	28.04.1993	Lisbon	Portuga	0–5	WCq
544	19.05.1993	Tallinn	Estonia	3–0	WCq
545	02.06.1993	Aberdeen	Estonia	3 1	WCq

546	08.09.1993	Aberdeen	Switzerland	1–1	WCq
547	13.10.1993	Rome	Italy	1–3	WCq
548	17.11.1993	Valletta	Malta	2–0	WCq
549	23.03.1994	Glasgow	Netherlands	0–1	
550	20.04.1994	Vienna	Austria	2–1	
551	27.05.1994	Utrecht	Netherlands	1–3	
552	07.09.1994	Helsinki	Finland	2–0	ECq
553	12.10.1994	Glasgow	Faroe Islands	5–1	ECq
554	16.11.1994	Glasgow	Russia	1–1	ECq
555	18.12.1994	Athens	Greece	0–1	
556	29.03.1995	Moscow	Russia	0–0	ECq
557	26.04.1995	Serravalle	San Marino	2–0	ECq
558	21.05.1995	Hiroshima	Japan	0–0	
559	25.05.1995	Toyama	Ecuador	2–1	
560	07.06.1995	Toftir	Faroe Islands	2–0	ECq
561	16.08.1995	Glasgow	Greece	1–0	ECq
562	06.09.1995	Glasgow	Finland	1–0	ECq
563	11.10.1995	Stockholm	Sweden	0–2	
564	15.11.1995	Glasgow	San Marino	5–0	ECq
565	27.03.1996	Glasgow	Australia	1–0	
566	24.04.1996	Copenhagen	Denmark	0–2	
567	26.05.1996	New Britain	United States	1–2	
568	29.05.1996	Miami	Colombia	0–1	
569	10.06.1996	Birmingham	Netherlands	0–0	EC
570	15.06.1996	Wembley	England	0–2	EC
571	18.06.1996	Birmingham	Switzerland	1–0	EC
572	31.08.1996	Vienna	Austria	0–0	WCq
573	05.10.1996	Riga	Latvia	2–0	WCq
574	10.11.1996	Glasgow	Sweden	1–0	WCq
575	11.02.1997	Monaco	Estonia	0–0	WCq
576	29.03.1997	Kilmarnock	Estonia	2–0	WCq
577	02.04.1997	Glasgow	Austria	2–0	WCq
578	30.04.1997	Gothenburg	Sweden	1–2	WCq
579	27.05.1997	Kilmarnock	Wales	0–1	
580	01.06.1997	Valletta	Malta	3–2	
581	08.06.1997	Minsk	Belarus	1–0	WCq

582	07.09.1997	Aberdeen	Belarus	4–1	WCq
583	11.10.1997	Glasgow	Latvia	2–0	WCq
584	12.11.1997	St Etienne	France	1–2	
585	25.03.1998	Glasgow	Denmark	0–1	
586	22.04.1998	Edinburgh	Finland	1–1	
587	30.05.1998	Washington	United States	0–0	
588	30.05.1998	New Jersey	Colombia	2–2	
589	10.06.1998	St Denis	Brazil	1–2	WC
590	16.06.1998	Bordeaux	Norway	1–1	WC
591	23.06.1998	St Etienne	Morocco	0–3	WC
592	05.09.1998	Vilnius	Lithuania	0–0	ECq
593	10.10.1998	Edinburgh	Estonia	3–2	ECq
594	14.10.1998	Aberdeen	Faroe Islands	2–1	ECq
595	31.03.1999	Glasgow	Czech Republic	1–2	ECq
596	28.04.1999	Bremen	Germany	1–0	
597	05.06.1999	Tórshavn	Faroe Islands	1–1	ECq
598	09.06.1999	Prague	Czech Republic	2–3	ECq
599	04.09.1999	Sarajevo	Bosnia	2–1	ECq
600	08.09.1999	Tallin	Estonia	0–0	ECq
601	05.10.1999	Glasgow	Bosnia	1–0	ECq
602	09.10.1999	Glasgow	Lithuania	3–0	ECq
603	13.11.1999	Glasgow	England	0–2	ECq
604	17.11.1999	Wembley	England	1–0	ECq

Played 92 Won 41 Drew 22 Lost 29

Thanks to Jostein Nygård for the above information.

Scottish Internationals born this day – 20 January
Thomas (Tommy) Wright (1928); James (Jimmy) Smith (1947);
John Neilson Robertson (1953); Colin Calderwood (1965)

— SGIAN DUBH QUOTE —

I'd like to get more caps under my belt.

Gary McAllister (57 caps)

— SALTIRE SEMINAR —

In the 1880s, English teams recruited heavily from north of the border. One of the most audacious examples of this 'poaching' was Stuart Macrae. He was capped five times for England, playing twice against Scotland, but was born at Port Bannatyne, Bute.

Scotland have played England 13 times in international challenge matches. Scotland won nine and lost only once

SCOTLAND v ENGLAND		
Hampden Park, Glasgow	14 Feb 1973	W 0–5
ENGLAND v SCOTLAND		
Bramall Lane, Sheffield	10 Mar 1883	W 2–3
SCOTLAND v ENGLAND		
1st Hampden Park, Glasgow	11 Mar 1882	W 5–1
ENGLAND v SCOTLAND		
Kennington Oval, London	12 Mar 1881	W 1–6
SCOTLAND v ENGLAND		
1st Hampden Park, Glasgow	13 Mar 1880	W 5–4
ENGLAND v SCOTLAND		
Kennington Oval, London	05 Apr 1879	L 5–4
SCOTLAND v ENGLAND		
1st Hampden Park, Glasgow	02 Mar 1878	W 7–2
ENGLAND v SCOTLAND		
Kennington Oval, London	03 Mar 1877	W 1–3
SCOTLAND v ENGLAND		
Hamilton Crescent, Glasgow	04 Mar 1876	W 3–0
ENGLAND v SCOTLAND		
Kennington Oval, London	06 Mar 1875	D 2–2
SCOTLAND v ENGLAND		
Hamilton Crescent, Glasgow	07 Mar 1874	W 2–1
ENGLAND v SCOTLAND		
Kennington Oval, London	08 Mar 1873	L 4–2
SCOTLAND v ENGLAND		
Hamilton Crescent, Glasgow	30 Nov 1872	D 0–0

Scottish Internationals born this day – 21 January
James Mitchell (1880);
Alexander Rooney (Alex) Forbes (1925); Alexander (Alex) McLeish (1959);
Douglas Alan (Dougie) Freedman (1974)

Scottish International born this day – 22 January
George Graham Aitken (1925)

— SGIAN DUBH QUOTE —

Reporter: *Gordon, do you think James Beattie deserves to be in the England squad?*
Strachan (50 caps): *I don't care, I'm Scottish.*

Scottish Internationals born this day – 23 January
John Johnstone (1869); James McDougall (1904);
Robert Denholm Baxter (1911); Thomas (Tom) Forsyth (1949);
Gary Mackay (1964)

Scottish Internationals born this day – 24 January
Robert Beattie (1916); Andrew (Andy) McLaren (1922);
William Russell Logan Bauld (1928); William (Willie) Henderson (1944);
Shaun Richard Maloney (1983)

— BARRY RAMMY – THE FIRST OFFICIAL INTERNATIONAL —

A crowd of about 4,000 gathered on 30 November 1872, a damp day at the West of Scotland Cricket Ground, Hamilton Crescent, Partick, Glasgow (which still exists and is used for cricket matches) to watch blue-clad Scotland kick 'up the brae'. Neither side scored but a disorganised England were fortunate to avoid defeat. One reporter told how: 'Individual skill was generally on England's side, but the Southrons did not play to each other as well as their opponents who seem to be adept in passing the ball. Perfect order was observed.'

The loudest cheer of the game was for Bob Leckie, who seemed to have scored, but the goal was not given as the ball was deemed by Scottish referee, William Keay, to have gone over the England tape (there were no crossbars then).

Glasgow Academicals had offered to let their ground be used for the game, but Partick staged the match at a cost of £10, which was paid to the cricket club. It was agreed that another £10 would be paid if over £50 was taken at the gate. In fact, paying customers handed over £103 to watch the match so it was a good day for cricket.

On that day, the Scots, all players from the Queen's Park club (although five also turned out for other clubs), wore blue jerseys with the red lion on the breast. Before the match, the weather prevented Scotland practising together, and the match came close to being postponed.

SCOTLAND	CLUB	CAPS	ENGLAND
Robert Gardner (Captain)	Queen's Park	1	Robert Barker
William Ker Greenhalgh	Queen's Park	1	Ernest Harwood
Joseph Taylor Welch	Queen's Park	1	Reginald de Courtenay
James J. Thomson	Queen's Park	1	Frederick Patey Chappell
James Smith	Queen's Park	1	William John Maynard
Robert Smith	Queen's Park	1	John Brockbank
Robert Leckie	Queen's Park	1	John Charles Clegg
Alex Rhind	Queen's Park	1	Arnold Kirke Smith
William MacKinnon	Queen's Park	1	John Ottaway (Captain)
James Weir Chenery	Queen's Park	1	Cuthbert Charles John
David Wotherspoon	Queen's Park	1	Charles John Morice

Referee: William Keay (Scotland)

Gardner, Ker and Thomson also played with Granville FC.

James and Robert Smith also played with South Norwood FC.

Scottish International born this day – 25 January
James Kennaway (1905)

— SGIAN DUBH QUOTE —

*Although we are playing Russian roulette, we are obviously
playing Catch 22 at the moment and it's a difficult scenario to
get my head round.*

Paul Sturrock (20 caps)

— BERSERKER BIOG – DR JOHN SMITH —

At 6ft 3in and weighing about 15 stone, Smith would have been a big man
in any era, but in his time he would have been considered a giant. Smith
ran out on to the soccer field 10 times for his country between 1877 and
1884. A useful forward, he netted a dozen goals for Scotland.

Born in Mauchline, Ayrshire, in 1855, Smith turned out for Mauchline,
Edinburgh University and Queen's Park during his career. He was educated
at Mauchline Parish School and Ayr Academy before taking up a place at
Edinburgh university where he became an all-round sportsman of repute,
while gaining his qualifications in medicine.

Initially an adherent of the rugby code, between 1874 and 1877 Smith
played for his University and in 1876 came close to being selected for the
Scottish national side. It was only the casting vote of the chairman that
blocked his taking up a full-back place.

Already an international player, in January 1879 Smith founded
Edinburgh University's association football club. He appeared 18 times and
scored seven goals for the Corinthians. One of these games was against
Blackburn Rovers in December 1884 when the famous amateur side
humiliated the Lancastrian English Cup holders 8–1. A year later, the
Scottish Football Association decreed that Smith would be disallowed from
playing against any Scottish club because he had turned out for the
Corinthians against Bolton Wanderers, a professional club.

Smith toured Australia with the Scottish rugby team in 1888, and in
1892 he refereed the Scotland v England soccer game.

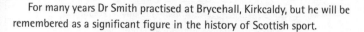
For many years Dr Smith practised at Brycehall, Kirkcaldy, but he will be remembered as a significant figure in the history of Scottish sport.

> **Scottish International born this day – 26 January**
> William Lennie (1882)

> **Scottish International born this day – 27 January**
> John Daniel Taylor (1872)

— SALTIRE SEMINAR —

Scotland's biggest win happened on 23 February 1901 at Celtic Park, Glasgow, when they beat Ireland 11–0 (scoring six goals in the second half; captain Bob Hamilton claimed four of that half-dozen).

> **Scottish International born this day – 28 January**
> David (Dave) McPherson (1964)

— SGIAN DUBH QUOTE —

Dave has this incredible knack of pulling a couple of chickens out of the hat each season.

Mark McGhee (4 caps 1983–84)

> **Scottish Internationals born this day – 29 January**
> Robert Bruce (1906); James Robert (Bobby) Combe (1924);
> David Hay (1948)

> **Scottish International born this day – 30 January**
> Andrew Cunningham (1891)

— SALTIRE SEMINAR —

Before the appointment of Bobby Brown in 1967 as Scotland's first manager, the Scottish XI was chosen by a selection committee consisting of up to 38 people.

Scottish Internationals born this day – 31 January
Patrick (Paddy) McCabe Buckley (1925);
James (Jim) Kennedy (1934); Alexander William (Alex) Hamilton (1939);
John Angus Paul Collins (1968)

— CALEDONIAN CHRONICLES —

In March 1873 Scotland were defeated 4–2 by England in London; however, there had been only enough money in the 'international fund' to buy eight return tickets to the capital for the Scottish side, so three of the team were London based: A.F. Kinnaird, H.W. Renny-Tailyour and J.E. Blackburn Kinnaird. The latter was born in London and later became an important figure in the English FA, but he qualified to play for Scotland because he owned land in Perthshire. Renny-Tailyour also represented Scotland at rugby union, although he had been born in India.

The gate receipts from the 3,000 spectators who watched the home side outclass their visitors were so good that both the English and the Scottish FAs (the latter was formed in 1873) would never again have difficulties in bringing 11 players to a game.

Player Name	Caps	Club	Goals	England	Goals
Robert Gardner (Captain)	2	Queen's Park		Alexander Morten (Cap)	
William Ker	2	Queen's Park		Ernest Harwood Greenhalgh	
Joseph Taylor	2	Queen's Park		Leonard Sidgwick Howell	
William Gibb	2	Queen's Park	60	Alfred George Goodwyn	
Robert Smith	2	Queen's Park		Pelham George von Donop	
David Wotherspoon	2	Queen's Park		Alexander George Bonsor	10
Henry Renny-Tailyour	1	Royal Engineers	25	William Edwin Clegg	
Arthur Kinnaird	1	The Wanderers		Robert Walpole Sealy Vidal	
John Blackburn	1	Royal Engineers		George Hubert Hugh Heron	
James J Thomson	1	Clydesdale		Charles John Chenery	85
William MacKinnon	2	Queen's Park		William Slanley Kenyon-Slaney	1,75

Referee: T. Lloyd (England)

Scottish International born this day – 1 February
Darren Barr Fletcher (1984)

— SGIAN DUBH QUOTE —

Reporter: *Gordon, you must be delighted with that result?*
Strachan: *You're spot on! You can read me like a book.*

Scottish Internationals born this day – 2 February
Daniel Blair (1906); James Anton Blyth (1955); Barry Ferguson (1978)

Scottish Internationals born this day – 3 February
William Gulliland (1871); Alexander (Alex) Young (1937);
John Angus McDonald Hansen (1950); Maurice Ross (1981)

— CALEDONIAN CHRONICLES —

Scotland have played England twice in the World Cup. Both were qualifying matches at Hampden Park. On 15 April 1950, Scotland lost 1–0 in front of 133,300 people. On 3 April 1954, a crowd of 134,544 saw England win 2–4 (Willie Ormond scored Scotland's second goal in the 89th minute).

Scottish International born this day – 4 February
James (Jimmy) Murray (1933)

— SALTIRE SEMINAR —

Scotland met England five times in the Rous Cup. They lost three and won just one, the last match played in this competition with the only goal of the game from Richard Gough.

SCOTLAND v ENGLAND		
Hampden Park, Glasgow	27 May 1989	L 0–2
ENGLAND v SCOTLAND		
Wembley Stadium, London	21 May 1988	L 1– 0
SCOTLAND v ENGLAND		
Hampden Park, Glasgow	23 May 1987	D 0–0
ENGLAND v SCOTLAND		
Wembley Stadium, London	23 Apr 1986	L 2–1
SCOTLAND v ENGLAND		
Hampden Park, Glasgow	25 May 1985	W 1–0

Scottish Internationals born this day – 5 February
Alexander (Alex) Forsyth (1952); William (Billy) Dodds (1969)

— SGIAN DUBH QUOTE —

We ended up playing football, and that's not our style.
Alex MacDonald (1 cap 1976)

Scottish International born this day – 6 February
John Murdoch (1901)

— BARRY RAMMY – THE FIRST OFFICIAL INTERNATIONAL VICTORY —

The international of 1874 was Scotland's first official victory. It was played at Hamilton Crescent, Glasgow, and watched by 7,000 spectators. Harry McNeil was carried shoulder-high from the field after the 2–1 triumph. The Scots' passing game relied less on the bouts of individual dribbling. This 'scientific football' would eventually be adopted throughout the game, but in 1874 the English found it hard to cope with. McNeil finessed Scotland back into the match following England's opening goal. Spectators went 'mad with delight' when the winning goal was scored.

SCOTLAND	CAPS	CLUB	GOALS	ENGLAND	GOALS
Robert Gardner	3	Clydesdale		Reginald de Courtenay Welch	
John Hunter MacIndoe Ogilvie	1	3rd Lanark Rifle Volunteers		Robert Andrew Muter	
Joseph Taylor	3	Queen's Park		Alfred Hugh Stratford	
James J. Thomson (Captain)	3	Queen's Park		Francis Hornby Birley	
Charles Campbell (Captain)	1	Queen's Park		Cuthbert John Ottaway	
James Weir Owen	2	Queen's Park		John Robert Blayney	
William MacKinnon	3	Queen's Park		Charles Henry Reynolds Wollaston	
John Ferguson Heron	1	Vale of Leven		George Hubert Hugh	
Angus McKinnon	1	Queen's Park	49	John Hawley Edwards	
Henry McNeil	1	Queen's Park		Robert Kennett Kingsford	28
Frederick Anderson	1	Clydesdale	43	Charles John Chenery	

Referee: Archibald Rae (Scotland)

Scottish Internationals born this day – 7 February
Thomas Bradshaw (1904); David Harvey (1948)

— SGIAN DUBH QUOTE —

I strongly feel that the only difference between the two teams were the goals that England scored.

Craig Brown (former Scotland manager)

Scottish International born this day – 8 February
Edward (Eddie) Rutherford (1921)

— CALEDONIAN CHRONICLES —

In 1875 Scotland were held to a draw by England. This was followed by a Scottish win. All the goals of the game were scored in the first half with the visitors unable to register. In 1876 Wales entered the international arena. Scotland proved their most difficult adversary for several years. The initial Scotland v Wales match attracted a crowd of approximately 20,000, and the Welsh lost 4–0 in Glasgow. Two years later, with just two days' notice, the Welsh FA wanted to cancel the game, as they were unable to raise a team. This would have meant that the Scottish Football Association would be out of pocket, having spent money on preparations and pre-match advertising. But William Dick, the Secretary of the Scottish FA, got on a train to Wrexham and toured a 40-mile radius of what was at that time the Welsh centre of soccer, and rounded up a side to play Scotland. The Welsh were beaten 9–0 (they were six down at the end of the first half); however, it was reported that they 'played a plucky game but were deficient in the passing and dodging tactics observed by some Scotsmen'.

It was five games before Wales scored a goal against Scotland.

Scotland dominated the early international era. Three weeks prior to their 9–0 win over Wales, England were destroyed 7–2 at Old Hampden on 2 March 1878. It was a windy day that had been preceded by two days of torrential rain. Scotland were 6–0 in front early in the second half. Four 'Macs' shared the goals (MacKinnon, McGregor, McDougall and McNeil).

England beat Scotland 5–4 in London in 1879 in an exciting game, but it was to be Scotland's only defeat in a run of 31 internationals between 8 March 1873 and 17 March 1888. The match had been arranged for 1 March, but it was postponed until Boat Race Day because of snow. England adopted the 'Scotch passing game' for the first time and C.W. Alcock, the Secretary of the English FA, hailed the contest as 'the finest international ever seen'.

Scotland were 4–1 in front at half-time, but Ted Bambridge's powerful run and shot won the game in the 83rd minute. Five minutes before this, with honours even at 4–4, Scotland had what seemed like a winning goal ruled offside by the English referee.

William Dick, the Secretary of the Scottish FA, said after that England

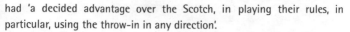

had 'a decided advantage over the Scotch, in playing their rules, in particular, using the throw-in in any direction'.

Scotland were accustomed to throw-ins being made in the direction of their own goal. Some games with Wales were played to the English/Welsh rules in the first half and the 'straight-throw' during the second. In Scotland/England games, this rule was an issue until a compromise was reached in 1882.

A Scottish referee presided over the Scotland v England game in 1880 and the home side won 5-4 in Glasgow. Three of the Scottish goals were disputed, but the Scots were 5-2 ahead when Charlie Campbell, having broken his jaw in a heading battle with England's Sam Widdowson, had to go off.

This was the start of a series of Scottish victories over England which included a 6-1 win at Kennington Oval. That remains England's heaviest home defeat by Scotland and the biggest inflicted by any country on England until Hungary won 1-7 at Wembley in 1954.

Scottish International born this day – 9 February
Gordon David Strachan (1957)

Scottish Internationals born this day – 10 February
Robert Frame Main (1909); Joseph (Joe) McDonald (1929);
William (Billy) Thomson (1958); Alan Bruce McInally (1963)

—— SGIAN DUBH QUOTE ——

Reporter: Gordon, can we have a quick word please?
Strachan: *Velocity!* [walks off]

Scottish International born this day – 11 February
George Key (1882)

SCOTLAND IN THE 1980s

Game No.	Date	Venue	Opponent	Score	Competition
426	26.03.1980	Glasgow	Portugal	4–1	ECq
427	17.05.1980	Belfast	Northern Ireland	0–1	HI
428	21.05.1980	Glasgow	Wales	1–0	HI
429	24.05.1980	Glasgow	England	0–2	HI
430	28.05.1980	Poznan	Poland	0–1	
431	31.05.1980	Budapest	Hungary	2–3	
432	10.09.1980	Stockholm	Sweden	1–0	WCq
433	15.10.1980	Glasgow	Portugal	0–0	WCq
434	25.02.1981	Tel Aviv	Israel	1–0	WCq
435	25.03.1981	Glasgow	Northern Ireland	1–1	WCq
436	28.04.1981	Glasgow	Israel	3–1	WCq
437	16.05.1981	Swansea	Wales	0–2	HI
438	19.05.1981	Glasgow	Northern Ireland	2–0	HI
439	23.05.1981	Wembley	England	1–0	HI
440	09.09.1981	Glasgow	Sweden	2–0	WCq
441	14.10.1981	Belfast	Northern Ireland	0–0	WCq
442	18.11.1981	Lisbon	Portugal	1–2	WCq
443	24.02.1982	Valencia	Spain	0–3	
444	23.03.1982	Glasgow	Netherlands	2–1	
445	28.04.1982	Belfast	Northern Ireland	1–1	HI
446	24.05.1982	Glasgow	Wales	1–0	HI
447	29.05.1982	Glasgow	England	0–1	HI
448	15.06.1982	Malaga	New Zealand	5–2	WC
449	18.06.1982	Seville	Brazil	1–4	WC
450	22.06.1982	Malaga	Soviet Union	2–2	WC
451	13.10.1982	Glasgow	East Germany	–0	ECq
452	17.11.1982	Berne	Switzerland	0–2	ECq
453	15.12.1982	Brussels	Belgium	2–3	ECq
454	30.03.1983	Glasgow	Switzerland	2–2	ECq
455	24.05.1983	Glasgow	Northern Ireland	0–0	HI
456	28.05.1983	Cardiff	Wales	2–0	HI
457	01.06.1983	Wembley	England	0–2	HI
458	12.06.1983	Vancouver	Canada	2–0	
459	16.06.1983	Edmonton	Canada	3–0	
460	20.06.1983	Toronto	Canada	2–0	
461	21.09.1983	Glasgow	Uruguay	2–0	
462	12.10.1983	Glasgow	Belgium	1–1	ECq
463	16.11.1983	Halle	East Germany	1–2	ECq
464	13.12.1983	Belfast	Northern Ireland	0–2	HI
465	28.02.1984	Glasgow	Wales	2–1	HI
466	26.05.1984	Glasgow	England	1–1	HI
467	01.06.1984	Marseilles	France	0–2	
468	12.09.1984	Glasgow	Yugoslavia	6–1	
469	17.10.1984	Glasgow	Iceland	3–0	WCq

470	14.11.1984	Glasgow	Spain	3–1	WCq
471	27.02.1985	Seville	Spain	0–1	WCq
472	27.03.1985	Glasgow	Wales	0–1	WCq
473	25.05.1985	Glasgow	England	1–0	
474	28.05.1985	Reykjavik	Iceland	1–0	WCq
475	10.09.1985	Cardiff	Wales	1–1	WCq
476	16.10.1985	Glasgow	East Germany	0–0	
477	20.11.1985	Glasgow	Australia	2–0	WCq
478	04.12.1985	Melbourne	Australia	0–0	WCq
479	28.01.1986	Tel Aviv	Israel	1–0	
480	26.03.1986	Glasgow	Romania	3–0	
481	23.04.1986	Wembley	England	1–2	
482	29.04.1986	Eindhoven	Netherlands	0–0	
483	04.06.1986	Nezahualcoyotl	Denmark	0–1	WC
484	08.06.1986	Queretaro	West Germany	1–2	WC
485	13.06.1986	Nezahualcoyotl	Uruguay	0–0	WC
486	10.09.1986	Glasgow	Bulgaria	0–0	ECq
487	15.10.1986	Dublin	Rep. of Ireland	0–0	ECq
488	12.11.1986	Glasgow	Luxembourg	3–0	ECq
489	18.02.1987	Glasgow	Rep. of Ireland	0–1	ECq
490	01.04.1987	Brussels	Belgium	1–4	ECq
491	23.05.1987	Glasgow	England	0–0	
492	26.05.1987	Glasgow	Brazil	0–2	
493	09.09.1987	Glasgow	Hungary	1–0	
494	14.10.1987	Glasgow	Belgium	2–0	ECq
495	11.11.1987	Sofia	Bulgaria	1–0	ECq
496	02.12.1987	Esch	Luxembourg	0–0	ECq
497	17.02.1988	Riyadh	Saudi Arabia	2–2	
498	22.03.1988	Valletta	Malta	1–1	
499	27.04.1988	Madrid	Spain	0–0	
500	17.05.1988	Glasgow	Colombia	0–0	
501	21.05.1988	Wembley	England	0–1	
502	14.09.1988	Oslo	Norway	2–1	WCq
503	19.10.1988	Glasgow	Yugoslavia	1–1	WCq
504	22.12.1988	Perugia	Italy	0–2	
505	08.02.1989	Limassol	Cyprus	3–2	WCq
506	08.03.1989	Glasgow	France	2–0	WCq
507	26.04.1989	Glasgow	Cyprus	2–1	WCq
508	27.05.1989	Glasgow	England	0–2	
509	30.05.1989	Glasgow	Chile	2–0	
510	06.09.1989	Zagreb	Yugoslavia	1–3	WCq
511	11.10.1989	Paris	France	0–3	WCq
512	15.11.1989	Glasgow	Norway	1–1	WCq

Played 87 Won 35 Drew 23 Lost 29

Thanks to Jostein Nygård for the above information.

— BERSERKER BIOG – PAUL JAMES HARTLEY —

Known as 'Zeko' in the game, Hartley was born in Glasgow on 19 October 1976 and started his career at Hamilton Academical in 1994. A £400,000 fee took him to Millwall in 1996 and it was during his season at the New Den that Paul consolidated his place in the Scotland Under-21 team. In 1997 Hartley joined Raith Rovers who paid £150,000 for his services and in 1998 he moved to Hibernian and helped the club win the Scottish First Division Championship in 1998/99.

During 1999/2000 Paul went on a brief loan to Greenock Morton. He hit home a free-kick against their deadly rivals St Mirren (whose supporters took a powerful dislike to Hartley, and, according to Paul, the feeling is mutual). Hartley played just three games for the Ton but is often seen in the Cappielow stands on match days.

Hartley joined St Johnstone in 2000 and, while at McDiarmid Park, Billy Stark, the manager of the Saints at the time, helped Hartley convert to a central midfielder (prior to this, he had played mainly as a peripheral winger). This resulted in a sharp improvement in Hartley's form and he returned to top-level competition in 2003, signing for Hearts on a free transfer when his contract expired.

A series of impressive performances resulted in Paul's first appearance for Scotland at Stadio Giuseppe Meazza Milano in a FIFA World Cup qualifier against Italy on 26 March 2005. It was a baptism of fire, and the home side won 2–0. Paul has subsequently won 14 more caps, scoring his first international goal in the Arena Petrol, Celje, during Scotland's 3–0 FIFA World Cup qualifier win over Slovenia on 12 October 2005.

During the January 2007 transfer window, Hartley was linked with possible moves to Rangers and Aston Villa, now managed by Martin O'Neill, who was behind an unsuccessful Celtic bid for the player in 2005. At the end of January 2007, Hartley joined the team he has supported since his boyhood at Celtic Park for a £1.1 million fee. He has Scottish Cup (2006) and Scottish First Division (1998/99) medals to his credit.

— SALTIRE SEMINAR —

In the first internationals, players didn't have numbers, so they wore different-coloured socks to identify each other.

Scottish International born this day – 12 February
William Thomas (Willie) Callaghan (1943)

— SGIAN DUBH QUOTE —

There's no way Ryan Giggs is another George Best. He's another Ryan Giggs.

Denis Law (55 caps)

Scottish International born this day – 13 February
Thomas Cochrane Highet (1853)

— BERSERKER BIOG – SCOTT BROWN —

Scott was born on 25 June 1985 in Dunfermline, Fife. During the 2003/04 season, he gained a reputation as a temperamental striker, with a propensity for collecting yellow cards. Having reinvented himself over the last few years, he has become a quality attacking midfielder and an influential member of the Hibernian team, nicknamed 'Broony' and 'Broonaldo' by Hibs fans.

Early in January 2007, it was reported Celtic Chief Executive Peter Lawwell was negotiating with Hibs with the aim of taking Brown to Glasgow, and in May of the same year he moved to Celtic Park for a record-breaking fee of £4.4 million.

Scott has been capped four times for the Scottish national team, and made his debut in a Hampden Park friendly against the USA in November 2005, after which he returned to the Under-21 squad, but was added to the full squad for the match with Lithuania in September 2006. Brown was selected for the full squad for the Euro 2008 qualifiers against France and Ukraine in October 2006, but was not called upon for either game. He is also one of the most highly rated up-and-coming young players in Scotland.

Scottish Internationals born this day – 14 February
John Ewart (1891); Hugh Howie (1924); William (Willie) Hunter (1940)

— CALEDONIAN CHRONICLES —

Scotland have met England five times in the UEFA European Championship. They have won two and lost two.

SCOTLAND V ENGLAND			
Hampden Park, Glasgow	Qualifier	24 Feb 1968	D 1–1
ENGLAND V SCOTLAND			
Wembley Stadium, London	Qualifier	15 Apr 1967	W 2–3
ENGLAND V SCOTLAND			
Wembley Stadium, London	Finals	15 Jun 1996	L 2–0
ENGLAND V SCOTLAND			
Wembley Stadium, London	Championship Play-off	17 Nov 1999	W 0–1
SCOTLAND V ENGLAND			
Hampden Park, Glasgow	Championship Play-off	13 Nov 1999	L 0–2

Scottish Internationals born this day – 15 February
Andrew Nesbit Wilson (1896); Scott Severin (1979)

— SALTIRE SEMINAR —

Scotland's biggest defeat happened on 19 June 1954 when they were beaten 7–0 in the St Jakob Stadium, Basle, Switzerland, by Uruguay in the FIFA World Cup. The unhappy keeper for Scotland that day was Fred Martin. It was his third international. His last cap, his sixth, was awarded for a Wembley meeting with England on 2 April 1955; 96,947 people saw him let in four goals in the first half and three in the second as Scotland were trounced 7–2.

> **Scottish Internationals born this day – 16 February**
> The Hon. (later Lord) Arthur Fitzgerald Kinnaird (1847);
> Ralph Allan Aitken (1863); Robert Young (Bobby) Collins (1931);
> William Murdoch (Willie) Hamilton (1938)

— CALEDONIAN CHRONICLES – THE FIRST CHAMPIONS —

In 1883/84, Ireland entered international competition. But Scotland were the first champions of what was to become the Home International Championship.

The Scotland v Ireland series began with the Scots hitting two goals in the first half. A seventh-minute opener by Dr Smith beat England at Cathkin Park before Scotland were shocked by the Welsh when a weakened Scottish side (Queen's Park were playing in the English Cup Final) went one down. But they equalised before the break through Joe Lindsay and went on to win comfortably in the second half with a brace from John Kay and a goal by Frank Shaw.

> **Scottish International born this day – 17 February**
> David Baird (1872)

> **Scottish Internationals born this day – 18 February**
> John Rae (Jock) Aird (1926); Steven Hammell (1982)

— SALTIRE SEMINAR —

For the 1887 match with England, Scotland adopted a man-for-man marking system in defence. Bob Kelso shadowed England's 'Prince of the Dribblers' William Cobbold. Kelso did such a good job that an English newspaper called him 'the Renton Ruffian'.

Scottish Internationals born this day – 19 February
Charles John (Charlie) Cox (1926);
Patrick Timothy (Pat/Paddy) Crerand (1939);
James Edward (Jim) McInally (1964);
Malcolm George (Malky) Mackay (1972)

Scottish Internationals born this day – 20 February
Andrew (Andy) Penman (1943); David Robert Speedie (1960)

— SGIAN DUBH QUOTE —

To be second with one game to go – you can't ask for more.
Stuart McCall (40 caps, 1990–98)

Scottish Internationals born this day – 21 February
Andrew Anderson (1909); John Bell Brown (1915);
John Carmichael (Johnny) Kelly (1921)

Scottish International born this day – 22 February
William Carruthers (Willie) Cunningham (1925)

— SALTIRE SEMINAR —

Scotland met England 85 times in the British Championship. Scotland won 30 and lost 35.

Scottish Internationals born this day – 23 February
Neil Gibson (1873); William Esplin (Willie) Ormond (1927)

Scottish Internationals born this day – 24 February
William Alexander (Willie) Fraser (1929); Denis Law (1940);
Brian Martin (1963); Neil Sullivan (1970)

SCOTLAND V ENGLAND		
Hampden Park, Glasgow	26 May 1984	D 1–1

SCOTLAND V ENGLAND		
Wembley Stadium, London	01 Jun 1983	L 0–2

SCOTLAND V ENGLAND		
Hampden Park, Glasgow	29 May 1982	L 0–1

ENGLAND V SCOTLAND		
Wembley Stadium, London	23 May 1981	L 0–1

SCOTLAND V ENGLAND		
Hampden Park, Glasgow	24 May 1980	L 0–2

ENGLAND V SCOTLAND		
Wembley Stadium, London	26 May 1979	L 3–1

SCOTLAND V ENGLAND		
Hampden Park, Glasgow	20 May 1978	L 0–1

ENGLAND V SCOTLAND		
Wembley Stadium, London	04 Jun 1977	W 1–2

SCOTLAND V ENGLAND		
Hampden Park, Glasgow	15 May 1976	W 2–1

ENGLAND V SCOTLAND		
Wembley Stadium, London	24 May 1975	W 5–1

SCOTLAND V ENGLAND		
Hampden Park, Glasgow	18 May 1974	W 2–0

ENGLAND V SCOTLAND		
Wembley Stadium, London	19 May 1973	L 1–0

SCOTLAND V ENGLAND		
Hampden Park, Glasgow	27 May 1972	L 0–1

ENGLAND V SCOTLAND		
Wembley Stadium, London	22 May 1971	L 3–1

SCOTLAND V ENGLAND		
Hampden Park, Glasgow	25 Apr 1970	D 0–0

ENGLAND V SCOTLAND		
Wembley Stadium, London	10 May 1969	L 4–1
SCOTLAND V ENGLAND		
Hampden Park, Glasgow	02 Apr 1966	L 3–4
ENGLAND V SCOTLAND		
Wembley Stadium, London	10 Apr 1965	D 2–2
SCOTLAND V ENGLAND		
Hampden Park, Glasgow	11 Apr 1964	W 1–0
ENGLAND V SCOTLAND		
Wembley Stadium, London	06 Apr 1963	W 1–2
SCOTLAND V ENGLAND		
Hampden Park, Glasgow	14 Apr 1962	W 2–0
ENGLAND V SCOTLAND		
Wembley Stadium, London	15 Apr 1961	L 9–3
SCOTLAND V ENGLAND		
Hampden Park, Glasgow	09 Apr 1960	D 1–1
ENGLAND V SCOTLAND		
Wembley Stadium, London	11 Apr 1959	L 1–0
SCOTLAND V ENGLAND		
Hampden Park, Glasgow	19 Apr 1958	L 0–4
ENGLAND V SCOTLAND		
Wembley Stadium, London	06 Apr 1957	L 2–1
SCOTLAND V ENGLAND		
Hampden Park, Glasgow	14 Apr 1956	D 1–1
ENGLAND V SCOTLAND		
Wembley Stadium, London	02 Apr 1955	L 7–2
ENGLAND V SCOTLAND		
Wembley Stadium, England	18 Apr 1953	D 2–2
SCOTLAND V ENGLAND		
Hampden Park, Glasgow	05 Apr 1952	L 1–2

ENGLAND V SCOTLAND		
Wembley Stadium, London	14 Apr 1951	W 2–3
SCOTLAND V ENGLAND (ENGLAND V SCOTLAND)		
Wembley Stadium, London	09 Apr 1949	W 1–3
SCOTLAND V ENGLAND		
Hampden Park, Glasgow	10 Apr 1948	L 0–2
ENGLAND V SCOTLAND		
Wembley Stadium London	12 Apr 1947	D 1–1
SCOTLAND V ENGLAND		
Hampden Park Glasgow	15 Apr 1939	L 1–2
ENGLAND V SCOTLAND		
Wembley Stadium, London	09 Apr 1938	W 0–1
SCOTLAND V ENGLAND		
Hampden Park, Glasgow	17 Apr 1937	W 3–1
ENGLAND V SCOTLAND		
Wembley Stadium, London	04 Apr 1936	D 1–1
SCOTLAND V ENGLAND		
Hampden Park, Glasgow	06 Apr 1935	W 2–0
ENGLAND V SCOTLAND		
Wembley Stadium, London	14 Apr 1934	L 3–0
SCOTLAND V ENGLAND		
Hampden Park, Glasgow	01 Apr 1933	W 2–1
ENGLAND V SCOTLAND		
Wembley Stadium, London	09 Apr 1932	L 3–0
SCOTLAND V ENGLAND		
Hampden Park, Glasgow	28 Mar 1931	W 2–0
ENGLAND V SCOTLAND		
Wembley Stadium, London	05 Apr 1930	L 5–2
SCOTLAND V ENGLAND		
Hampden Park, Glasgow	13 Apr 1929	W 1–0

ENGLAND V SCOTLAND		
Wembley Stadium London	31 Mar 1928	W 1–5
SCOTLAND V ENGLAND		
Hampden Park, Glasgow	02 Apr 1927	L 1–2
ENGLAND V SCOTLAND		
Old Trafford, Manchester	17 Apr 1926	W 0–1
SCOTLAND V ENGLAND		
Hampden Park, Glasgow	04 Apr 1925	W 2–0
ENGLAND V SCOTLAND		
Wembley Stadium, London	12 Apr 1924	D 1–1
SCOTLAND V ENGLAND		
Hampden Park, Glasgow	14 Apr 1923	D 2–2
ENGLAND V SCOTLAND		
Villa Park, Birmingham	08 Apr 1922	W 0–1
SCOTLAND V ENGLAND		
Hampden Park, Glasgow	09 Apr 1921	W 3–0
ENGLAND V SCOTLAND		
Hillsborough, Sheffield	10 Apr 1920	L 5–4
SCOTLAND V ENGLAND		
Hampden Park, Glasgow	04 Apr 1914	W 3–1
ENGLAND V SCOTLAND		
Stamford Bridge, London	05 Apr 1913	L 1–0
SCOTLAND V ENGLAND		
Hampden Park, Glasgow	23 Mar 1912	D 1–1
ENGLAND V SCOTLAND		
Goodison Park, Liverpool	01 Apr 1911	D 1–1
SCOTLAND V ENGLAND		
Hampden Park, Glasgow	02 Apr 1910	W 2–0
ENGLAND V SCOTLAND		
Crystal Palace, London	03 Apr 1909	L 2–0

SCOTLAND V ENGLAND		
Hampden Park, Glasgow	04 Apr 1908	D 1-1
ENGLAND V SCOTLAND		
St James' Park, Newcastle	06 Apr 1907	D 1-1
SCOTLAND V ENGLAND		
Hampden Park, Glasgow	07 Apr 1906	W 2-1
ENGLAND V SCOTLAND		
Crystal Palace, London	01 Apr 1905	L 1-0
SCOTLAND V ENGLAND		
Celtic Park, Glasgow	09 Apr 1904	L 0-1
ENGLAND V SCOTLAND		
Bramall Lane, Sheffield	04 Apr 1903	W 1-2
ENGLAND V SCOTLAND		
Villa Park, Birmingham	03 May 1902	D 2-2
ENGLAND V SCOTLAND		
Crystal Palace, London	30 Mar 1901	D 2-2
SCOTLAND V ENGLAND		
Celtic Park, Glasgow	07 Apr 1900	W 4-1
ENGLAND V SCOTLAND		
Villa Park, Birmingham	08 Apr 1899	L 2-1
SCOTLAND V ENGLAND		
Celtic Park, Glasgow	02 Apr 1898	L 1-3
ENGLAND V SCOTLAND		
Crystal Palace, London	03 Apr 1897	W 1-2
SCOTLAND V ENGLAND		
Celtic Park, Glasgow	04 Apr 1896	W 2-1
ENGLAND V SCOTLAND		
Goodison Park, Liverpool	06 Apr 1895	L 3-0
SCOTLAND V ENGLAND		
Celtic Park, Glasgow	07 Apr 1894	D 2-2

ENGLAND V SCOTLAND		
Richmond Athletic Ground, London 01 Apr 1893		L 5–2
SCOTLAND V ENGLAND		
Ibrox Park, Glasgow	02 Apr 1892	L 1–4
ENGLAND V SCOTLAND		
Ewood Park, Blackburn	04 Apr 1891	L 2–1
SCOTLAND V ENGLAND		
2nd Hampden Park, Glasgow	05 Apr 1890	D 1–1
ENGLAND V SCOTLAND		
Kennington Oval, London	13 Apr 1889	W 2–3
SCOTLAND V ENGLAND		
1st Hampden Park, Glasgow	17 Mar 1888	L 0–5
ENGLAND V SCOTLAND		
Leamington Road, Blackburn	19 Mar 1887	W 2–3
SCOTLAND V ENGLAND		
1st Hampden Park, Glasgow	27 Mar 1886	D 1–1
ENGLAND V SCOTLAND		
Kennington Oval, London	21 Mar 1885	D 1–1
SCOTLAND V ENGLAND		
1st Cathkin Park, Glasgow	15 Mar 1884	W 1–0

Overall, of the 110 games played between Scotland and England between 1872 and January 2007, Scotland have won 42 and been defeated 43 times.

— BERSERKER BIOG – ANDREW WATSON —

Born in May 1857 in Demerara, British Guiana, Watson was the world's first black international football player. He would play three times for Scotland between 1881 and 1882 and was amongst the dozen most significant of the 19th century.

The son of Peter Miller, a wealthy Scottish sugar planter, and Rose Watson, a Guianese woman, Andrew was sent to London and Kings College at 14. When he was 19, he studied philosophy, mathematics and engineering at the University of Glasgow, where his passion for football bloomed. He was an excellent sportsman.

Watson played for Maxwell FC in 1876 and then joined local side Parkgrove FC where he also took on the role of match secretary, making him football's first recorded black administrator. He married in Glasgow and signed for Queen's Park FC, at that time Britain's leading football club. He led the side to several Scottish Cup victories, making himself the first black player to win a major competition football medal.

Able to play on the left or right side of the defence or midfield, Watson won three international caps for Scotland.

In 1882, Andrew gained the distinction of being the first black player to play in the FA Cup when he ran out for London Swifts FC. In 1884, he was the first player from overseas to be invited to join the Corinthians FC who were created to challenge the supremacy of Queen's Park and the Scottish national side, and, using only the very best players, allowed themselves just 50 members.

It has often been claimed that the first recorded black footballer was Arthur Wharton, but it was recently noted that Watson was playing 11 years prior to Wharton. Unlike Wharton, Watson was always an amateur. This mistake was probably perpetuated as no written records or match reports have been found that mention Watson's skin colour. However, one reporter did make allusions to Watson and colour, writing about his unusual brown boots (football boots were traditionally black at the time). But Watson's colour seems to have had no impact on those he played with and against and there is no record of him experiencing racism, discrimination or prejudice.

Watson's entry in the *Scottish Football Association Annual* of 1880-81 says, 'Watson, Andrew: One of the very best backs we have; since joining

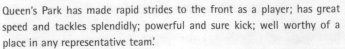

Queen's Park has made rapid strides to the front as a player; has great speed and tackles splendidly; powerful and sure kick; well worthy of a place in any representative team.'

Little is know about Watson after he left Scottish football. He emigrated to Australia, and he died in Sydney where he is buried.

In 1926 'Tityrus' (J.A.H. Catton, a famous and respected sports writer and editor of the *Athletic News*) selected Andrew as left-back in his all-time Scotland team. This was a truly amazing approbation of the skill and gifts of a player from such an early era of the game by an esteemed observer of football who had seen most if not every England/Scotland international over the previous half-century.

Scottish Internationals born this day – 25 February
David (Davie) Cooper (1956); Alistair (Ally) Dawson (1958)

Scottish Internationals born this day – 26 February
Thomas Breckenridge (1865); Thomas Brandon (1869);
Michael James Stewart (1981)

Scottish International born this day – 27 February
Alexander McGeoch (1855)

Scottish International born this day – 28 February
James Blessington (1874)

— CALEDONIAN CHRONICLES —

SCOTLAND IN THE 1970s

Game No.	Date	Venue	Opponent	Score	Competition
337	18.04.1970	Belfast	Northern Ireland	1–0	HI
338	22.04.1970	Glasgow	Wales	0–0	HI
339	25.04.1970	Glasgow	England	0–0	HI
340	11.11.1970	Glasgow	Denmark	1–0	ECq
341	03.02.1971	Liège	Belgium	0–3	ECq
342	21.04.1971	Lisbon	Portugal	0–2	ECq
343	18.05.1971	Glasgow	Northern Ireland	0–1	
344	22.05.1971	Wembley	England	1–3	
345	09.06.1971	Copenhagen	Denmark	0–1	ECq
346	14.06.1971	Moscow	Soviet Union	0–1	
347	13.10.1971	Glasgow	Portugal	2–1	ECq
348	10.11.1971	Aberdeen	Belgium	1–0	ECq
349	15.11.1971	Cardiff	Wales	0–0	
350	01.12.1971	Rotterdam	Netherlands	1–2	
351	26.04.1972	Glasgow	Peru	2–0	
352	20.05.1972	Glasgow	Northern Ireland	2–0	HI
353	24.05.1972	Glasgow	Wales	1–0	HI
354	27.05.1972	Glasgow	England	0–1	HI
355	29.06.1972	Belo Horizonte	Yugoslavia	2–2	
356	02.07.1972	Porto Alegre	Czechoslovakia	0–0	
357	05.07.1972	Rio de Janeiro	Brazil	0–1	
358	18.10.1972	Copenhagen	Denmark	4–1	WCq
359	15.11.1972	Glasgow	Denmark	2–0	WCq
360	14.02.1973	Glasgow	England	0–5	
361	12.05.1973	Wrexham	Wales	2–0	HI
362	16.05.1973	Glasgow	Northern Ireland	1–2	HI
363	19.05.1973	Wembley	England	0–1	HI
364	22.06.1973	Berne	Switzerland	0–1	
365	30.06.1973	Glasgow	Brazil	0–1	
366	26.09.1973	Glasgow	Czechoslovakia	2–1	WCq
367	17.10.1973	Prague	Czechoslovakia	0–1	WCq
368	14.11.1973	Glasgow	West Germany	1–1	

369	05.02.1974	Valencia	Spain	1–1	ECq
370	27.03.1974	Frankfurt	West Germany	1–2	
371	11.05.1974	Glasgow	Northern Ireland	0–1	HI
372	14.05.1974	Glasgow	Wales	2–0	HI
373	18.05.1974	Wembley	England	2–0	HI
374	02.06.1974	Brussels	Belgium	1–2	
375	06.06.1974	Oslo	Norway	2–1	
376	14.06.1974	Dortmund	Zaire	2–0	WC
377	18.06.1974	Frankfurt	Brazil	0–0	WC
378	22.06.1974	Frankfurt	Yugoslavia	1–1	WC
379	30.10.1974	Glasgow	East Germany	3–0	
380	20.11.1974	Glasgow	Spain	1–2	ECq
381	16.04.1975	Gothenburg	Sweden	1–1	
382	13.05.1975	Glasgow	Portugal	1–0	
383	17.05.1975	Cardiff	Wales	2–2	HI
384	20.05.1975	Glasgow	Northern Ireland	3–0	HI
385	24.05.1975	Wembley	England	1–5	HI
386	01.06.1975	Bucharest	Romania	1–1	ECq
387	03.09.1975	Copenhagen	Denmark	1–0	ECq
388	29.10.1975	Glasgow	Denmark	3–1	ECq
389	17.12.1975	Glasgow	Romania	1–1	ECq
390	07.04.1976	Glasgow	Switzerland	1–0	
391	06.05.1976	Glasgow	Wales	3–1	HI
392	08.05.1976	Glasgow	Northern Ireland	3–0	HI
393	15.05.1976	Glasgow	England	2–1	HI
394	08.09.1976	Glasgow	Finland	6–0	
395	13.10.1976	Prague	Czechoslovakia	0–2	WCq
396	17.11.1976	Glasgow	Wales	1–0	WCq
397	27.04.1977	Glasgow	Sweden	3–1	
398	28.05.1977	Wrexham	Wales	0–0	HI
399	01.06.1977	Glasgow	Northern Ireland	3–0	HI
400	04.06.1977	Wembley	England	2–1	HI
401	15.06.1977	Santiago	Chile	4–2	
402	18.06.1977	Buenos Aires	Argentina	1–1	
403	23.06.1977	Rio de Janeiro	Brazil	0–2	
404	21.09.1977	Glasgow	Czechoslovakia	3–1	WCq

405	07.10.1977	Berlin	East Germany	0–1	
406	12.10.1977	Liverpool	Wales	2–0	WCq
407	22.02.1978	Glasgow	Bulgaria	2–1	
408	13.05.1978	Belfast	Northern Ireland	1–1	HI
409	17.05.1978	Glasgow	Wales	1–1	HI
410	20.05.1978	Glasgow	England	0–1	HI
411	03.06.1978	Cordoba	Peru	1–3	WC
412	07.06.1978	Cordoba	Iran	1–1	WC
413	11.06.1978	Mendoza	Netherlands	3–2	WC
414	20.09.1978	Vienna	Austria	2–3	ECq
415	25.10.1978	Glasgow	Norway	3–2	ECq
416	29.11.1978	Lisbon	Portugal	0–1	ECq
417	19.05.1979	Cardiff	Wales	0–3	HI
418	22.05.1979	Glasgow	Northern Ireland	1–0	HI
419	26.05.1979	Wembley	England	1–3	HI
420	02.06.1979	Glasgow	Argentina	1–3	
421	07.06.1979	Oslo	Norway	4–0	ECq
422	12.09.1979	Glasgow	Peru	1–1	
423	17.10.1979	Glasgow	Austria	1–1	ECq
424	21.11.1979	Brussels	Belgium	0–2	ECq
425	19.12.1979	Glasgow	Belgium	1–3	ECq

Played 89 Won 34 Drew 20 Lost 35

Thanks to Jostein Nygård for the above information.

— SGIAN DUBH QUOTE —

The one thing I didn't expect is the way we didn't play.

George Graham (12 caps)

> **Scottish International born this day – 29 February**
> Thomas C. Vallance (1856)

> **Scottish Internationals born this day – 1 March**
> Robert (Bobby) Ferguson (1945); George Connolly (1949)

— DISCIPLINE —

Fifteen players have been sent off while playing for Scotland. Only two have left the field during a home game. A Scottish player is most likely to be sent off in a World Cup qualifying match, away from home, against Eastern European opponents. More players have been sent off playing for Scotland since 1981 than in all the rest of the nation's footballing history.

PLAYER	DATE	OPPONENTS	COMPETITION	STADIUM
Billy Steel	27 May 1951	Austria	Challenge Match	Prater Stadium, Vienna
Robert (Bertie) Auld	27 May 1959	Netherlands	Challenge Match	Olympic Stadium, Amsterdam
Pat Crerand	14 May 1961	Czechoslovakia	World Cup Qualifier	Tehelne Pole Stadium, Bratislava
Tommy Gemmell	22 Oct 1969	West Germany	World Cup Qualifier	Volkspark Stadium, Hamburg
Peter Lorimer	15 Nov 1972	Denmark	World Cup Qualifier	Hampden Park, Glasgow
Andy Gray	13 Oct 1976	Czechoslovakia	World Cup Qualifier	Sparta Stadium, Prague
Willie Johnston	18 Jun 1977	Argentina	Challenge Match	Buenos Aires
Joe Jordan	16 May 1981	Wales	British International Championship	Vetch Field, Swansea
Richard Gough	09 Sep 1992	Switzerland	World Cup Qualifier	Wankdorf Stadium, Berne
John Spencer	21 May 1995	Japan	Kirin Cup	Big Arch Stadium, Hiroshima
Craig Burley	23 Jun 1998	Morocco	World Cup Finals	Stade Geoffroy-Guichard, St Etienne
Matt Elliott	05 Jun 1999	Faroe Islands	European Championship Qualifier	Toftir Stadium, Toftir
Maurice Ross	10 Sep 2003	Germany	European Championship Qualifier	Westfalenstadion Dortmund
James McFadden	09 Oct 2004	Norway	World Cup Qualifier	Hampden Park, Glasgow
Steven Pressley	11 Oct 2006	Ukraine	European Championship Qualifier	Olympic Stadium, Kiev

— BOOKINGS —

Thirty-two Scottish players have been booked more than twice; 70 more have been booked once or twice. Bertie Auld, Pat Crerand, Tommy Gemmell, Peter Lorimer and Billy Steel were sent off without first being booked.

PLAYER	NO. OF BOOKINGS	PLAYER	NO. OF BOOKINGS
Christian Dailly	12	Graeme Souness	4
Gary Caldwell	9	Steven Thompson	4
James McFadden	8	Martin Buchan	3
Steven Pressley	7	Stephen Crawford	3
Barry Ferguson	7	Willie Donachie	3
Andy Gray	7	Darren Fletcher	3
Kevin Gallacher	6	Colin Hendry	3
Don Hutchison	6	Allan Johnston	3
Joe Jordan	6	Lee McCulloch	3
Colin Calderwood	5	Danny McGrain	3
John Collins	5	Gordon McQueen	3
Gary Naysmith	5	Kenny Miller	3
Callum Davidson	4	Nigel Quashie	3
Paul Dickov	4	Maurice Ross	3
Darren Jackson	4	Andy Webster	3
Stuart McCall	4	David Weir	3

Scottish International born this day – 2 March
William (Billy) McNeill (1940)

Scottish International born this day – 3 March
William (Willie) Thornton (1920)

Scottish International born this day – 4 March
Kenneth Mathieson (Kenny) Dalglish (1951)

Scottish International born this day – 5 March
David Marshall (1985)

Scottish International born this day – 6 March
Martin McLean Buchan (1949)

— SALTIRE SEMINAR —

The McCall brothers, Jim and Archie, were two of four Renton players who withdrew from the Scottish team scheduled to meet Ireland in 1892. Jim, the elder brother, had been named as skipper of the side. The two would never be in the same international team.

Scottish International born this day – 7 March
William (Willie) Waddell (1921)

Scottish International born this day – 8 March
John McGregor (1851)

Scottish International born this day – 9 March
Ernest (Ernie) McGarr (1944); James Garven (Jim) Stewart (1954);
Gary James Holt (1973)

— SGIAN DUBH QUOTE —

He's one of those footballers whose brains are in his head.

Derek Johnstone (14 caps)

— CALEDONIAN CHRONICLES —

SCOTLAND IN THE 1960s					
Game No.	Date	Venue	Opponent	Score	Competition
273	19.04.1960	Glasgow	England	1–1	HI
274	29.05.1960	Vienna	Austria	1–4	
275	04.06.1960	Glasgow	Poland	2–3	
276	05.06.1960	Budapest	Hungary	3–3	
277	08.06.1960	Ankara	Turkey	2–4	
278	20.10.1960	Cardiff	Wales	0–2	HI
279	09.11.1960	Glasgow	Northern Ireland	5–2	HI
280	15.04.1961	Wembley	England	3–9	HI
281	03.05.1961	Glasgow	Rep. of Ireland	4–1	WCq

282	07.05.1961	Dublin	Rep. of Ireland	3–0	WCq
283	14.05.1961	Bratislava	Czechoslovakia	0–4	WCq
284	26.09.1961	Glasgow	Czechoslovakia	3–2	WCq
285	07.10.1961	Belfast	Northern Ireland	6–1	
286	08.11.1961	Glasgow	Wales	2–0	
287	29.11.1961	Brussels	Czechoslovakia	2–4	WCq
288	14.04.1962	Glasgow	England	2–0	HI
289	02.05.1962	Glasgow	Uruguay	2–3	
290	20.10.1962	Cardiff	Wales	3–2	HI
291	07.11.1962	Glasgow	Northern Ireland	5–1	HI
292	06.04.1963	Wembley	England	2–1	HI
293	08.05.1963	Glasgow	Austria	4–1	
294	04.06.1963	Bergen	Norway	3–4	
295	09.06.1963	Dublin	Rep. of Ireland	0–1	
296	13.06.1963	Madrid	Spain	6–2	
297	12.10.1963	Belfast	Northern Ireland	1–2	HI
298	07.11.1963	Glasgow	Norway	6–1	
299	20.11.1963	Glasgow	Wales	2–1	HI
300	11.04.1964	Glasgow	England	1–0	HI
301	12.05.1964	Hanover	West Germany	2–2	
302	03.10.1964	Cardiff	Wales	2–3	HI
303	21.10.1964	Glasgow	Finland	3–1	WCq
304	25.11.1964	Glasgow	Northern Ireland	3–2	HI
305	10.04.1965	Wembley	England	2–2	HI
306	08.05.1965	Glasgow	Spain	0–0	
307	23.05.1965	Chorzow	Poland	1–1	WCq
308	27.05.1965	Helsinki	Finland	2–1	WCq
309	02.10.1965	Belfast	Northern Ireland	2–3	HI
310	13.10.1965	Glasgow	Poland	1–2	WCq
311	09.11.1965	Glasgow	Italy	1–0	WCq
312	24.11.1965	Glasgow	Wales	4–1	HI
313	07.12.1965	Naples	Italy	0–3	WCq
314	02.04.1966	Glasgow	England	3–4	HI
315	11.05.1966	Glasgow	Netherlands	0–3	
316	18.06.1966	Glasgow	Portugal	0–1	
317	25.06.1966	Glasgow	Brazil	1–1	

318	22.10.1966	Cardiff	Wales	1–1	ECq
319	16.11.1966	Glasgow	Northern Ireland	2–1	
320	15.04.1967	Wembley	England	3–2	ECq
321	10.05.1967	Glasgow	Soviet Union	0–2	
322	21.10.1967	Belfast	Northern Ireland	0–1	
323	22.11.1967	Glasgow	Wales	3–2	
324	24.01.1968	Glasgow	England	1–1	ECq
325	30.05.1968	Amsterdam	Netherlands	0–0	
326	16.10.1968	Copenhagen	Denmark	1–0	
327	06.11.1968	Glasgow	Austria	2–1	WCq
328	17.12.1968	Nicosia	Cyprus	5–0	WC
329	16.04.1969	Glasgow	West Germany	1–1	WCq
330	03.05.1969	Wrexham	Wales	5–3	HI
331	06.05.1969	Glasgow	Northern Ireland	1–1	HI
332	10.05.1969	Wembley	England	1–4	HI
333	11.05.1969	Glasgow	Cyprus	8–0	WCq
334	21.09.1969	Dublin	Rep. of Ireland	1–1	
335	22.10.1969	Hamburg	West Germany	2–3	WCq
336	05.11.1969	Vienna	Austria	0–2	WCq

Played 64 Won 27 Drew 13 Lost 24

Thanks to Jostein Nygård for the above information.

Scottish Internationals born this day – 10 March
Henry Smith (1956); David (Dave) Bowman (1960); Neil Alexander (1978)

Scottish Internationals born this day – 11 March
William Blair (1872); David Provan (1941); David Steel Stewart (1947); John Brownlie (1952)

— SALTIRE SEMINAR —

129 players have captained Scotland but only 18 have skippered the side 10 times or more.

CAPTAIN	NO.	FIRST AND LAST CAPTAINCY
George Young	48	April 1948 – May 1957
Billy Bremner	39	November 1968 – September 1975
Gary McAllister	31	September 1993 – March 1999
Roy Aitken	26	October 1986 – June 1990
Graeme Souness	26	May 1982 – June 1986
Barry Ferguson	22	September 2003 – June 2007
Archie Gemmill	22	May 1976 – March 1981
Colin Hendry	22	May 1996 – March 2001
Paul Lambert	16	October 1999 – September 2003
John Greig	15	December 1965 – October 1975
Eric Caldow	14	October 1960 – April 1963
James Simpson	13	November 1934 – May 1937
Charles Thomson	13	April 1905 – April 1913
Christian Dailly	12	May 2002 – November 2005
Bobby Evans	12	June 1958 – June 1960
William Ferguson Miller	11	June 1983 – October 1988
Danny McGrain	10	May 1980 – June 1982
Bruce Rioch	10	May 1977 – June 1978

Scottish International born this day – 12 March
James Lang (1851)

Scottish Internationals born this day – 13 March
Henry Miller Morris (1919); Alexander Bryce (Alex) Linwood (1920)

— BARRY RAMMY – A BAD DAY IN GLASGOW —

On 17 March 1888, having been watched by a crowd of 10,000, England left Glasgow with their first away win in Scotland. It was the first loss suffered by Scotland since 5 April 1879 and their first-ever home defeat; it ended an extraordinary series of 19 matches and nine years without an international loss.

The St Patrick's Day debacle at the Old Hamden Park saw England leading 4–0 at half-time. John Goodall, a Londoner by birth but brought up in Kilmarnock, in the traditions of Scottish football, was probably the visitors' most effective player.

SCOTLAND	GAPS	CLUB	ENGLAND	GOALS
John Lindsay	1	Renton	William Robert Moon	
Walter Arnott	9	Queen's Park	Robert Henry Howarth	
Donald Gow (Captain)	1	Rangers	Percy Melmoth Walters	
Robert Kelso	1	Renton	Henry Allen	
James Kelly	5	Dumbarton	George Haworth	
Leitch Keir	6	Renton	Cecil Henry Holden-White	
Alexander Hamilton	4	Queen's Park	George Woodhall	
William Berry	1	Queen's Park	John Goodall	43
William Sellar	5	Battlefield	Dr Tinsley Lindley (Captain)	32
James McCall	4	Renton	Dennis Hodgetts	34
John Lambie	3	Queen's Park	Frederick Dewhurst	40;49

Referee: John Sinclair (Ireland)

Scottish International born this day – 14 March
Hugh Baird (1930)

The experiment of meeting Wales at Easter Road was seen as a success and only the talent and courage of the Welsh keeper, Jimmy Trainer, of Preston North End, limited Scotland to five goals.

Gillespie and Hughes couldn't make it to Belfast for the game with Ireland, but they weren't needed. Scotland were 7–2 up coming out for the second half, thanks in great part to substandard Irish goalkeeping. Strangely for the period, the Irish keeper wore a different-coloured jersey to those of the rest of the team. Some commentators of the time suggested that this was indicative of the Irish being 'untogether'.

Scottish Internationals born this day – 15 March
John (Jock) Buchanan (1899); Ian Ferguson (1967)

— SGIAN DUBH QUOTE —

I was saying the other day, how often the most vulnerable area for goalies is between their legs.

Andy Gray (20 caps), Sky Sport

Scottish International born this day – 16 March
Thomas Usher (Tommy) Pearson (1913)

Scottish Internationals born this day – 17 March
John Cunningham (1930);
Lawrence Grant (Lawrie) Leslie (1935);
Alexander (Alex) MacDonald (1948);
Francis Peter (Frank) McGarvey (1956)

— SALTIRE SEMINAR —

In the early days of football, the game had officials known as 'umpires'. They usually made the decisions and only appealed to the referee when there was a difference of opinion. The two umpires for the Scotland v Ireland match of 1889 were both Scottish and both named John Campbell, although they weren't related.

Scottish Internationals born this day – 18 March
Robert Brown (1860); Hugh Wilson (1869);
John Livingstone (Ian) McMillan (1931);
Charles (Charlie) Miller (1976); Kris Boyd (1983)

Scottish Internationals born this day – 19 March
James Howie (1878); Robert (Bobby) Brown (1923);
John Dick (1930)

— SALTIRE SEMINAR —

Twenty players have captained Scotland more than five but less than ten times.

PLAYER	NO.	PLAYER	NO.
Sandy Jardine	9	James McMullan	6
Charles Campbell	8	David Meiklejohn	6
Tommy Docherty	8	Jock Shaw	6
Richard Gough	8	Thomas Boyd	5
Alex McLeish	8	Willie Cunningham	5
Billy McNeill	8	Denis Law	5
Kenny Dalglish	7	Alec McNair	5
Dave Mackay	7	William McStay	5
Paul McStay	7	Alex Raisbeck	5
Bobby Moncur	7	Gordon Strachan	5

Scottish International born this day – 20 March
Ian Murray (1981)

— CALEDONIAN CHRONICLES —

SCOTLAND IN THE 1950s

Game No.	Date	Venue	Opponent	Score	Competition
206	15.04.1950	Glasgow	England	0–1	WCq/HI
207	26.04.1950	Glasgow	Switzerland	3–1	
208	21.05.1950	Lisbon	Portugal	2–2	
209	27.05.1950	Paris	France	1–0	
210	21.10.1950	Cardiff	Wales	3–1	HI
211	01.11.1950	Glasgow	Northern Ireland	6–1	HI
212	13.12.1950	Glasgow	Austria	0–1	
213	14.04.1951	Wembley	England	3–2	HI
214	12.05.1951	Glasgow	Denmark	3–1	
215	16.05.1951	Glasgow	France	1–0	
216	20.05.1951	Brussels	Belgium	5–0	
217	27.05.1951	Vienna	Austria	0–4	
218	06.10.1951	Belfast	Northern Ireland	3–0	HI
219	14.11.1951	Glasgow	Wales	0–1	HI

220	05.04.1952	Glasgow	England	1–2	HI
221	30.04.1952	Glasgow	United States	6–0	
222	25.05.1952	Copenhagen	Denmark	2–1	
223	30.05.1952	Stockholm	Sweden	1–3	
224	05.11.1952	Glasgow	Northern Ireland	1–1	HI
225	18.11.1952	Cardiff	Wales	2–1	HI
226	18.04.1953	Wembley	England	2–2	HI
227	06.05.1953	Glasgow	Sweden	1–2	
228	03.10.1953	Belfast	Northern Ireland	3–1	WCq/HI
229	04.11.1953	Glasgow	Wales	3–3	WCq/HI
230	03.04.1954	Glasgow	England	2–4	WCq/HI
231	05.05.1954	Glasgow	Norway	1–0	
232	19.05.1954	Oslo	Norway	1–1	
233	25.05.1954	Helsinki	Finland	2–1	
234	16.06.1954	Zürich	Austria	0–1	WC
235	19.06.1954	Basle	Uruguay	0–7	WC
236	16.10.1954	Cardiff	Wales	1–0	HI
237	03.11.1954	Glasgow	Northern Ireland	2–2	HI
238	08.12.1954	Glasgow	Hungary	2–4	
239	02.04.1955	Wembley	England	2–7	HI
240	04.05.1955	Glasgow	Portugal	3–0	
241	15.05.1955	Belgrade	Yugoslavia	2–2	
242	19.05.1955	Vienna	Austria	4–1	
243	29.05.1955	Budapest	Hungary	1–3	
244	08.10.1955	Belfast	Northern Ireland	1–2	HI
245	09.11.1955	Glasgow	Wales	2–0	HI
246	14.04.1956	Glasgow	England	1–1	HI
247	02.05.1956	Glasgow	Austria	1–1	
248	20.10.1956	Cardiff	Wales	2–2	HI
249	07.11.1956	Glasgow	Northern Ireland	1–0	HI
250	21.11.1956	Glasgow	Yugoslavia	2–0	
251	06.04.1957	Wembley	England	1–2	HI
252	08.05.1957	Glasgow	Spain	4–2	WCq
253	19.05.1957	Basle	Switzerland	2–1	WCq
254	22.05.1957	Stuttgart	West Germany	3–1	
255	26.05.1957	Madrid	Spain	1–4	WCq
256	05.10.1957	Belfast	Northern Ireland	1–1	HI

257	06.11.1957	Glasgow	Switzerland	3–2	WCq
258	13.11.1957	Glasgow	Wales	1–1	HI
259	19.04.1958	Glasgow	England	0–4	HI
260	07.05.1958	Glasgow	Hungary	1–1	
261	01.06.1958	Warzaw	Poland	2–1	
262	08.06.1958	Västeras	Yugoslavia	1–1	WC
263	11.06.1958	Norrköping	Paraguay	2–3	WC
264	15.06.1958	Örebro	France	1–2	WC
265	05.11.1958	Glasgow	Northern Ireland	2–2	HI
266	18.11.1958	Cardiff	Wales	3–0	HI
267	11.04.1959	Wembley	England	0–1	HI
268	06.05.1959	Glasgow	West Germany	3–2	
269	27.05.1959	Amsterdam	Netherlands	2–1	
270	03.06.1959	Lisbon	Portugal	0–1	
271	03.10.1959	Belfast	Northern Ireland	4–0	HI
272	04.11.1959	Glasgow	Wales	1–1	HI

Played 67 Won 30 Drew 15 Lost 22

Thanks to Jostein Nygård for the above information.

Scottish International born this day – 21 March
James (Jimmy) Wardhaugh (1929)

Scottish International born this day – 22 March
James Hamilton Speirs (1886)

Scottish Internationals born this day – 23 March
William Telfer (1909); Robert (Bertie) Auld (1938)

— SGIAN DUBH QUOTE —

We threw our dice into the ring and turned up trumps.

Bruce Rioch (24 caps)

Scottish International born this day – 24 March
Archibald (Archie) Gemmill (1947)

Scottish International born this day – 25 March
Philip (Phil) O'Donnell (1972)

— SGIAN DUBH QUOTE —

It's an incredible rise to stardom. At 17 you're more likely to get a call from Michael Jackson than Sven Goran Eriksson.
Gordon Strachan (referring to Wayne Rooney)

Scottish International born this day – 26 March
Peter Wilson (1926)

Scottish Internationals born this day – 27 March
Ian Henderson Black (1924);
Ronald Michael (Ronnie) Glavin (1951);
Ian William Wilson (1958)

— SALTIRE SEMINAR —

In 1890 when Scotland met Ireland, the Scottish side wore their usual dark-blue shirts, but about half the team wore dark-blue bottoms and the remainder were in white shorts.

Scottish International born this day – 28 March
John McDougall (1853)

Scottish International born this day – 29 March
David George Black (1868);
Robert Findlay (1877);
Robert Bryson Templeton (1880);
Edmund Peter Skiruing (Eddie) Colquhoun (1945)

— SALTIRE SEMINAR —

Eighteen players have captained Scotland between three and four times.

PLAYER	NO.	PLAYER	NO.
Andrew Anderson	4	Jimmy Blair	3
James Curran Baxter	4	William Cringan	3
James Crapnell	4	John Gillespie	3
John Drummond	4	Asa Hartford	3
James Kelly	4	James Hay	3
Jim Leighton	4	David Morris	3
David Weir	4	Thomas Robertson	3
Thomas Younger	4	John T Robertson	3
Walter Arnott	3	Pat Stanton	3

Scottish International born this day – 30 March
John Gilchrist (1899); John Martis (1940)

Scottish International born this day – 31 March
David Richmond Gardner (1873); James (Jim) Forrest (1927)

Scottish International born this day – 1 April
Thomas Law (1928)

— SGIAN DUBH QUOTE —

Without picking out anyone in particular, I thought Mark Wright was tremendous.

Graeme Souness (54 caps)

Scottish International born this day – 2 April
Archibald F Devine (1887)

Scottish International born this day – 3 April
John Hughes (1943)

— SALTIRE SEMINAR —

Twenty-one players have captained Scotland twice.

Captains

David Davidson	James McAulay
George Brown	John C.M. McPherson
Martin Buchan	Robert Neill
Darren Fletcher	Michael Paton
Robert Gardner	Donald Currie Sillars
George Gillespie	Robert Smellie
Robert Hamilton	Gordon Smith
David Hay	Nicol Smith
John Marshall	James Stark
Alex Massie	Joseph Taylor
Don Masson	

Scottish International born this day – 4 April
William (Billy) Houliston (1921)

Scottish Internationals born this day – 5 April
Alfred James (Alfie) Conn Jnr. (1952);
Charles Richard (Richard) Gough (1962)

— CALEDONIAN CHRONICLES —

SCOTLAND IN THE 1940S

Game No.	Date	Venue	Opponent	Score	Competition
189	19.10.1946	Wrexham	Wales	1–3	HI
190	27.11.1946	Glasgow	Northern Ireland	0–0	HI
191	12.04.1947	Wembley	England	1–1	HI
192	18.05.1947	Brussels	Belgium	1–2	
193	24.05.1947	Luxembourg	Luxembourg	6–0	
194	04.10.1947	Belfast	Northern Ireland	0–2	HI
195	12.11.1947	Glasgow	Wales	1–2	HI
196	10.04.1948	Glasgow	England	0–2	HI

197	28.04.1948	Glasgow	Belgium	2–0	
198	17.05.1948	Berne	Switzerland	1–2	
199	23.05.1948	Paris	France	0–3	
200	23.10.1948	Cardiff	Wales	3–1	HI
201	17.11.1948	Glasgow	Northern Ireland	3–2	HI
202	09.04.1949	Wembley	England	3–1	HI
203	27.04.1949	Glasgow	France	2–0	
204	01.10.1949	Belfast	Northern Ireland	8–2	WCq/HI
205	09.11.1949	Glasgow	Wales	2–0	WCq/HI

Played 17 Won 8 Drew 2 Lost 7

Thanks to Jostein Nygård for the above information.

Scottish Internationals born this day – 6 April
Neil Mochan (1927); Andrew Francis (Andy) Walker (1965)

Scottish International born this day – 7 April
Alexander Brown (1879)

— SGIAN DUBH QUOTE —

With news of Scotland's 0–0 victory over Holland ...

Scottish TV

Scottish Internationals born this day – 8 April
William (Billy) Dickson (1945); John McGinlay (1964)

Scottish International born this day – 9 April
John Inglis (1859)

— SALTIRE SEMINAR —

Only seven capped players were included in the 1929 Scottish tour of Europe, but the expedition was a huge success. In the Grunewaldstadion, Berlin, over 40,000 people came to see Germany play out a 1–1 draw with

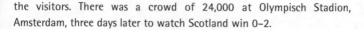
the visitors. There was a crowd of 24,000 at Olympisch Stadion, Amsterdam, three days later to watch Scotland win 0–2.

Scottish Internationals born this day – 10 April
John Knight (Jackie) Mudie (1930); Thomas (Tommy) Younger (1930)

Scottish International born this day – 11 April
Samuel Thomson (1862)

— SGIAN DUBH QUOTE —

Football has taken the place of religion in Scotland.

Robin Jenkins (Scottish author)

— SALTIRE SEMINAR —

Fifty-four players have captained Scotland once.

Captains

Maurice Malpas	John Hutton
Danny Blair	Thomas Alexander Jackson
Craig Burley	John Johnstone
John Campbell	Robert Robison Kelso
Kenneth Campbell	John Alexander Lambie
James Cowan	Henry James Hall Marshall
Sammy Cox	Robert W. Marshall
Thomas Craig	Ally McCoist
Andrew Cunningham	John McDougall
James Dougall	James McDougall
Tom Forsyth	Peter McGonagle
Kevin Gallacher	James McLaren
Neil Gibson	John McLeod
James Gordon	Frank McLintock
Paul Hegarty	Jackie McNamara
John Hill	Gordon McQueen
Andrew Holm	Peter McWilliam

Alan Morton
Thomas Muirhead
Peter Nellies
James Oswald
Steven Pressley
John Ritchie
Archibald Rowan
Matthew Scott
William Sellar
William Semple

David Shaw
Duncan Stewart
David Storrier
James J Thomson
Andrew Thomson
Thomas Townsley
Andrew Watson
Andrew Nesbit Wilson
Willie Woodburn

Scottish International born this day – 12 April
Gary Caldwell (1982)

Scottish Internationals born this day – 13 April
John Cameron (1872); Samuel Richardson (Sammy) Cox (1924);
James Fergus (Jim) Cruickshank (1941); Maurice (Mo) Johnston (1963);
Andrew Lewis (Andy) Goram (1964)

— SGIAN DUBH QUOTE —

Last night we were the best team on the day.

Roy Aitken (57 caps)

Scottish Internationals born this day – 14 April
Paul John Devlin (1972); James McFadden (1983)

Scottish Internationals born this day – 15 April
John May (1878); David George Herd (1934);
Edward Graham (Eddie) McCreadie (1940)

— SALTIRE SEMINAR —

In 1892, David Baird (Hearts) was selected to play against Wales, and Alex Keillor (Montrose) against the Irish. The players decided to exchange places as each had already played against those countries and wanted a different cap.

Scottish International born this day – 16 April
Archibald (Archie) Glen (1929)

Scottish International born this day – 17 April
John Gow (1869)

Scottish International born this day – 18 April
Eamonn John Bannon (1958)

Scottish Internationals born this day – 19 April
William (Willie) Moir (1922); Gordon George Banks Marshall (1964)

Scottish International born this day – 20 April
Lee Wilkie (1980)

Scottish Internationals born this day – 21 April
Thomas James Jenkinson (1865); Thomas Bingham (Tommy) Orr (1924)

— SALTIRE SEMINAR —

During Scotland's 1935 tour of North America, an American journalist called Tommy Walker 'the Babe Ruth of British soccer', a title they had already given to Andy Wilson in 1921. Scotland were victorious in all 13 of their games on that tour, including 5–1 and 4–1 slaughters of the United States. In the first match, at the New York Polo Grounds, which drew the biggest US soccer crowd for nine years, only a marvellous performance by Stanley Chesney, the 6ft 4in American keeper, limited the score to single figures.

Scottish International born this day – 22 April
William (Billy) McKinlay (1969)

Scottish Internationals born this day – 23 April
George Horsburgh Allan (1875); Frank Brennan (1924);
Andrew (Andy) Webster (1982)

— CALEDONIAN CHRONICLES —

SCOTLAND IN THE 1930S

Game No.	Date	Venue	Opponent	Score	Competition
148	22.02.1930	Glasgow	Northern Ireland	3–1	HI
149	05.04.1930	Wembley	England	2–5	HI
150	18.05.1930	Paris	France	2–0	
151	25.10.1930	Glasgow	Wales	1–1	HI
152	21.02.1931	Belfast	Northern Ireland	0–0	HI
153	28.03.1931	Glasgow	England	2–0	HI
154	16.05.1931	Vienna	Austria	0–5	
155	20.05.1931	Rome	Italy	0–3	
156	24.05.1931	Geneva	Switzerland	3–2	
157	19.09.1931	Glasgow	Northern Ireland	3–1	HI
158	31.10.1931	Wrexham	Wales	3–2	HI
159	09.04.1932	Wembley	England	0–3	HI
160	08.05.1932	Paris	France	3–1	
161	12.09.1932	Belfast	Northern Ireland	4–0	HI
162	26.10.1932	Edinburgh	Wales	2–5	HI
163	01.04.1933	Glasgow	England	2–1	HI
164	16.09.1933	Glasgow	Northern Ireland	1–2	HI
165	04.10.1933	Cardiff	Wales	2–3	HI
166	29.11.1933	Glasgow	Austria	2–2	
167	14.04.1934	Wembley	England	0–3	HI
168	20.10.1934	Belfast	Northern Ireland	1–2	HI
169	21.11.1934	Aberdeen	Wales	3–2	HI
170	06.04.1935	Glasgow	England	2–0	HI
171	05.10.1935	Cardiff	Wales	1–1	HI
172	13.11.1935	Edinburgh	Northern Ireland	2–1	HI
173	04.04.1936	Wembley	England	1–1	HI
174	14.10.1936	Glasgow	Germany	2–0	
175	31.10.1936	Belfast	Northern Ireland	3–1	HI
176	02.12.1936	Dundee	Wales	1–2	HI
177	17.04.1937	Glasgow	England	3–1	HI
178	09.05.1937	Vienna	Austria	1–1	
179	22.05.1937	Prague	Czechoslovakia	3–1	

180	30.10.1937	Cardiff	Wales	1–2	HI
181	10.11.1937	Aberdeen	Northern Ireland	1–1	HI
182	08.12.1937	Glasgow	Czechoslovakia	5–0	
183	09.04.1938	Wembley	England	1–0	HI
184	21.05.1938	Amsterdam	Netherlands	3–1	
185	08.10.1938	Belfast	Northern Ireland	2–0	HI
186	09.11.1938	Edinburgh	Wales	3–2	HI
187	07.12.1938	Glasgow	Hungary	3–1	
188	15.04.1939	Glasgow	England	1–2	HI

Played 41 Won 22 Drew 7 Lost 12

Thanks to Jostein Nygård for the above information.

Scottish Internationals born this day – 24 April
Thomas Henderson (Tommy) Docherty (1928);
Robert (Rob) Douglas (1972);
Dominic Matteo (1974)

Scottish International born this day – 25 April
Scott Brown (1985)

— SGIAN DUBH QUOTE —

Ally MacLeod thinks that tactics are a new kind of mint.
Glaswegian, pseudo-proletarian 'comedian'/stereotype-riding, banana-footed Billy Connolly (on infamous Scotland soccer manager Ally MacLeod)

Scottish Internationals born this day – 26 April
Patrick (Pat) Quinn (1936); Jamie McAllister (1978)

Scottish Internationals born this day – 27 April
Andrew 'Daddler' Aitken (1877); Adam McLean (1899)

— CALEDONIAN CHRONICLES —

SCOTLAND IN THE 1920s

Game No.	Date	Venue	Opponent	Score	Competition
114	26.02.1920	Cardiff	Wales	1–1	HI
115	13.03.1920	Glasgow	Ireland	3–0	HI
116	10.04.1920	Sheffield	England	4–5	HI
117	12.02.1921	Aberdeen	Wales	2–1	HI
118	26.02.1921	Belfast	Northern Ireland	2–0	HI
119	09.04.1921	Glasgow	England	3–0	HI
120	04.02.1922	Wrexham	Wales	1–2	HI
121	04.03.1922	Glasgow	Northern Ireland	2–1	HI
122	08.04.1922	Aston Villa	England	1–0	HI
123	03.03.1923	Belfast	Northern Ireland	1–0	HI
124	17.03.1923	Glasgow	Wales	2–0	HI
125	14.04.1923	Glasgow	England	2–2	HI
126	16.02.1924	Cardiff	Wales	0–2	HI
127	01.03.1924	Glasgow	Northern Ireland	2–0	HI
128	12.04.1924	Wembley	England	1–1	HI
129	14.02.1925	Edinburgh	Wales	3–1	HI
130	28.02.1925	Belfast	Northern Ireland	3–0	HI
131	04.04.1925	Glasgow	England	2–0	HI
132	31.10.1925	Cardiff	Wales	3–0	HI
133	27.02.1926	Glasgow	Northern Ireland	4–0	HI
134	17.04.1926	Manchester	England	1–0	HI
135	30.10.1926	Glasgow	Wales	3–0	HI
136	26.02.1927	Belfast	Northern Ireland	2–0	HI
137	02.04.1927	Glasgow	England	1–2	HI
138	29.10.1927	Wrexham	Wales	2–2	HI
139	25.02.1928	Glasgow	Northern Ireland	0–1	HI
140	31.03.1928	Wembley	England	5–1	HI
141	27.10.1928	Glasgow	Wales	4–2	HI
142	23.02.1929	Belfast	Northern Ireland	7–3	HI
143	13.04.1929	Glasgow	England	1–0	HI
144	26.05.1929	Bergen	Norway	7–3	
145	01.06.1929	Berlin	Germany	1–1	
146	04.06.1929	Amsterdam	Netherlands	2–0	
147	26.10.1929	Cardiff	Wales	4–2	HI

Played 34 Won 24 Drew 5 Lost 6

Thanks to Jostein Nygård for the above information.

— SGIAN DUBH QUOTE —

Wayne Rooney really has a man's body on a teenager's head.
George Graham (12 caps)

Scottish International born this day – 28 April
John Anderson White (1937)

Scottish International born this day – 29 April
James Murray Boyd (1907)

— SALTIRE SEMINAR —

Dave Camming, Scotland's keeper, together with his defenders, held England off in April 1938. He kept a clean sheet but it was Dave's only cap in peacetime.

Scottish Internationals born this day – 30 April
John Edward Blackburn (1851); David Steel Allan (1863)

Scottish Internationals born this day – 1 May
William (Billy) Steel (1923); Douglas (Doug) Cowie (1926); Daniel Fergus (Danny) McGrain (1950); John Doyle (1951)

Scottish International born this day – 2 May
William Ferguson (Willie) Miller (1955)

— SGIAN DUBH QUOTE —

This would cut hooliganism in half by 75 per cent.
Tommy Docherty (25 caps and former Scotland manager)

Scottish International born this day – 3 May
James Niven (1862)

> **Scottish International born this day – 4 May**
> Alexander Troup (1895)

> **Scottish Internationals born this day – 5 May**
> George Turner Livingston (or Livingstone) (1870);
> David (Dave) Shaw (1917); Robert Campbell (Campbell) Forsyth (1939);
> Derek James Parlane (1953)

— SALTIRE SEMINAR —

Scotland's 1939 close season tour of North America concluded with a record of 13 wins in 14 games, with one match drawn. An encounter in Vancouver was played under floodlights, and a game with the American League marked the first time that a Scottish side had to play extra-time. Another 30 minutes were played following a 2–2 draw in normal time. Jimmy Carabine, who had scored an equaliser, completed his hat-trick to help Scotland to a 4–2 victory.

Two notable achievements during the tour were Archie Garrett's seven goals in St Louis and, after trailing 1–0 in Detroit at half-time to a Michigan team, Scotland fought back to win 7–1.

> **Scottish Internationals born this day – 6 May**
> George Herd (1936); Graeme James Souness (1953)

> **Scottish Internationals born this day – 7 May**
> George (Dod) Brewster (1893); William (Willie) McNaught (1922);
> James Philip (Jim) Craig (1943); Garry O'Connor (1983)

— SALTIRE SEMINAR —

On 14 April 1945, Tommy Bogan of Scotland crashed into Frank Swift, the English keeper, in Scotland's first attack in the game. As a consequence, Tommy's international career lasted for about one minute and he didn't even manage to touch the ball while wearing a Scotland shirt. He left the field with knee-ligament damage.

Scottish International born this day – 8 May
George Mulhall (1936); David Alexander (Davie) Provan (1956)

Scottish International born this day – 9 May
Donald (Don) Hutchinson (1971)

Scottish Internationals born this day – 10 May
Colin Stein (1947); James Grady (Jim) Brown (1952);
David Gillespie (Davie) Weir (1970)

— CALEDONIAN CHRONICLES —

SCOTLAND IN THE 1910s

Game No.	Date	Venue	Opponent	Score	Competition
99	05.03.1910	Kilmarnock	Wales	1–0	HI
100	19.03.1910	Belfast	Ireland	0–1	HI
101	02.04.1910	Glasgow	England	2–0	HI
102	06.03.1911	Cardiff	Wales	2–2	HI
103	18.03.1911	Glasgow	Ireland	2–0	HI
104	01.04.1911	Everton	England	1–1	HI
105	02.03.1912	Edinburgh	Wales	1–0	HI
106	16.03.1912	Belfast	Ireland	4–1	HI
107	23.03.1912	Glasgow	England	1–1	HI
108	03.03.1913	Wrexham	Wales	0–0	HI
109	15.03.1913	Dublin	Ireland	2–1	HI
110	05.04.1913	Chelsea	England	0–1	HI
111	28.02.1914	Glasgow	Wales	0–0	HI
112	14.03.1914	Belfast	Ireland	1–1	HI
113	4.04.1914	Glasgow	England	3–1	HI

Played 15 Won 7 Drew 6 Lost 2

Thanks to Jostein Nygård for the above information.

Scottish Internationals born this day – 11 May
James Blair (1888); James Grady Brown (1952)

— SALTIRE SEMINAR —

In August 1946, Scotland drew 2–2 with England at Maine Road, Manchester, in a game played in aid of the Bolton Disaster Fund. Stanley Matthews laid on two first-half goals for Welsh, while Waddell created two for Thornton after the interval. This was one of only four occasions when Rangers' famous and feared Waddell/Thornton combination was on show in a Scotland team.

Scotland: Miller (Celtic); D. Shaw (Hibernian), J. Shaw (Rangers), Campbell (Morton), Brennan (Newcastle U), Husband (Partick T), Waddell (Rangers), Dougal (Birmingham C), Thornton (Rangers), Hamilton (Aberdeen), Liddell (Liverpool).

> **Scottish Internationals born this day – 12 May**
> Walter Arnott (1863); John Henderson Blackley (1948)

> **Scottish Internationals born this day – 13 May**
> Fred Martin (1929); Samuel (Sammy) Baird (1930); John Clark (1941)

— SGIAN DUBH QUOTE —

One thing about Germany – they'll be organised, they'll be big, and they'll be strong.

Ally McCoist (61 caps and former International assistant manager/coach)

> **Scottish Internationals born this day – 14 May**
> Eric Caldow (1934); Thomas (Tommy) Lawrence (1940);
> Joseph (Joe) Craig (1954); Lee Henry McCulloch (1978)

> **Scottish International born this day – 15 May**
> James Brownlie (1885)

— SALTIRE SEMINAR —

On 28 May 1947, Scotland played the British Army on the Rhine in Germany. George Young, playing centre-forward, opened the scoring but Scotland lost 4–3. They were thwarted by a goalkeeper soon to be a Scottish star, Jimmy Cowan. Pearson scored the other two Scottish goals.

The team was: Miller; Shaw (D), Shaw (J), Brown, Woodburn, Husband, MacFarlane, Flavell, Young, Steel, Pearson.

Scottish Internationals born this day – 16 May
Thomas Usher Pearson (1913); Robert (Bobby) Watson (1946)

Scottish International born this day – 17 May
Keith Wright (1965)

— SGIAN DUBH QUOTE —

He was in a no-win situation, unless he won the match.

Murdo MacLeod (20 caps)

Scottish International born this day – 18 May
Lee Miller (1983)

— BERSERKER BIOG – NICOL SMITH —

An awesome tackler, swift to recover, and possessing a potent shoulder-charge, Smith played for Scotland a dozen times between 1897 and 1902. A right-back, born in Darvel, Ayrshire, in 1873, his club career started with Darvel but he later moved to Rangers and set up a celebrated partnership with Jock Drummond; however, surprisingly, the two rarely appeared together in the Scottish international side. Nichol spent 12 years with Rangers before his tragic death from enteric fever in January 1905 aged just 31. From the same lace-making town as his namesake Alec, a later Scottish International, Nicol played his first international game in 1896, giving a powerful performance for the Scottish League against the Football League.

— CALEDONIAN CHRONICLES —

SCOTLAND IN THE 1900s

Game No.	Date	Venue	Opponent	Score	Competition
69	03.02.1900	Aberdeen	Wales	5–2	HI
70	03.03.1900	Belfast	Ireland	3–0	HI
71	07.04.1900	Glasgow	England	4–1	HI
72	23.02.1901	Glasgow	Ireland	11–0	HI
73	02.03.1901	Wrexham	Wales	1–1	HI
74	30.03.1901	Crystal Palace	England	2–2	HI
75	01.03.1902	Belfast	Ireland	5–1	HI
76	15.03.1902	Greenock	Wales	5–1	HI
77	03.05.1902	Birmingham	England	2–2	HI
78	09.03.1903	Cardiff	Wales	1–0	HI
79	21.03.1903	Glasgow	Ireland	0–2	HI
80	04.04.1903	Sheffield	England	2–1	HI
81	12.03.1904	Dundee	Wales	1–1	HI
82	26.03.1904	Dublin	Ireland	1–1	HI
83	09.04.1904	Glasgow	England	0–1	HI
84	06.03.1905	Wrexham	Wales	1–3	HI
85	18.03.1905	Glasgow	Ireland	4–0	HI
86	01.04.1905	Crystal Palace	England	0–1	HI
87	03.03.1906	Edinburgh	Wales	0–2	HI
88	17.03.1906	Dublin	Ireland	1–0	HI
89	07.04.1906	Glasgow	England	2–1	HI
90	04.03.1907	Wrexham	Wales	0–1	HI
91	16.03.1907	Glasgow	Ireland	3–0	HI
92	06.04.1907	Newcastle	England	1–1	HI
93	07.03.1908	Dundee	Wales	2–1	HI
94	14.03.1908	Dublin	Ireland	5–0	HI
95	04.04.1908	Glasgow	England	1–1	HI
96	01.03.1909	Wrexham	Wales	2–3	HI
97	15.03.1909	Glasgow	Ireland	5–0	HI
98	03.04.1909	Crystal Palace	England	0–2	HI

Played 30 Won 15 Drew 6 Lost

Thanks to Jostein Nygård for the above information.

> **Scottish International born this day – 19 May**
> Torrance Gillick (1915)

> **Scottish International born this day – 20 May**
> Mark Edward McGhee (1957)

— SALTIRE SEMINAR —

When Scotland won 3–1 at Wembley in 1949, the game came to be known as 'Cowan's Match' and the heroic Scottish goalkeeper was carried through crowds of elated fans. He eventually limped to the dressing room, fell on to a bench and said, 'Oh, Lord, save us from our friends!'

> **Scottish International born this day – 21 May**
> Walter Campbell Allison Aitkenhead (1887)

> **Scottish International born this day – 22 May**
> John Blair (1910)

> **Scottish Internationals born this day – 23 May**
> Ian Andrew Wallace (1956); Stephen Glass (1976)

> **Scottish Internationals born this day – 24 May**
> Douglas (Doug) Rougvie (1956); Brian Irvine (1965)

> **Scottish International born this day – 25 May**
> Gordon Smith (1924)

— CALEDONIAN CHRONICLES —

SCOTLAND IN THE 1890s

Game No.	Date	Venue	Opponent	Score	Competition
39	22.03.1890	Glasgow	Wales	5–0	HI
40	29.03.1890	Belfast	Ireland	4–1	HI
41	05.04.1890	Glasgow	England	1–1	HI
42	21.03.1891	Wrexham	Wales	4–3	HI
43	28.03.1891	Glasgow	Ireland	2–1	HI
44	06.04.1891	Blackburn	England	1–2	HI
45	19.03.1892	Belfast	Ireland	3–2	HI
46	26.03.1892	Edinburgh	Wales	6–1	HI
47	02.04.1892	Glasgow	England	1–4	HI
48	18.03.1893	Wrexham	Wales	8–0	HI
49	25.03.1893	Glasgow	Ireland	6–1	HI
50	01.04.1893	Richmond	England	2–5	HI
51	24.03.1894	Kilmarnock	Wales	5–2	HI
52	31.03.1894	Belfast	Ireland	2–1	HI
53	07.04.1894	Glasgow	England	2–2	HI
54	23.03.1895	Wrexham	Wales	2–2	HI
55	30.03.1895	Glasgow	Ireland	3–1	HI
56	06.04.1895	Blackburn	England	0–3	HI
57	21.03.1896	Dundee	Wales	4–0	HI
58	28.03.1896	Belfast	Ireland	3–3	HI
59	04.04.1896	Glasgow	England	2–1	HI
60	20.03.1897	Wrexham	Wales	2–2	HI
61	27.03.1897	Glasgow	Ireland	5–1	HI
62	03.04.1897	Crystal Palace	England	2–1	HI
63	19.03.1898	Motherwell	Wales	5–2	HI
64	26.03.1898	Belfast	Ireland	3–0	HI
65	02.04.1898	Glasgow	England	1–3	HI
66	18.03.1899	Wrexham	Wales	6–0	HI
67	25.03.1899	Glasgow	Ireland	9–1	HI
68	08.04.1899	Birmingham	England	1–2	HI

Played 30 Won 19 Drew 5 Lost 6

Thanks to Jostein Nygård for the above information.

— SALTIRE SEMINAR —

Scotland sailed to America in 1949, aboard the *Queen Mary*. The Scots lost only one game, but that was a dramatic upset. At Triborough Stadium, in front of 15,000 spectators, Belfast Celtic held on to their 2–0 interval lead. The other eight games were won and amongst the more positive features of the tour were Willie Waddell's six goals in Philadelphia, a floodlit game against St Louis All-Stars, and a 4–0 win over the United States. The following year, the Americans beat England in the World Cup.

Scottish Internationals born this day – 26 May
Matthew (Matt) Busby (1909); George Tomlinson McLean (1943)

Scottish International born this day – 27 May
Davidson Berry (1875)

Scottish Internationals born this day – 28 May
John (Jackie) Husband (1918); George Gilbert Miller Aitken (1925)

Scottish International born this day – 29 May
James Main (1886)

— CALEDONIAN CHRONICLES —

SCOTLAND IN THE 1880s

Game No.	Date	Venue	Opponent	Score	Competition
13	13.03.1880	Glasgow	England	5–4	
14	03.04.1880	Glasgow	Wales	5–1	
15	12.03.1881	Kennington Oval	England	6–1	
16	14.03.1881	Wrexham	Wales	5–1	
17	11.03.1882	Glasgow	England	5–1	
18	25.03.1882	Glasgow	Wales	5–0	
19	10.03.1883	Sheffield	England	3–2	
20	12.03.1883	Wrexham	Wales	4–1	
21	26.01.1884	Belfast	Ireland	5–0	HI
22	15.03.1884	Glasgow	England	1–0	HI
23	29.03.1884	Glasgow	Wales	4–1	HI
24	14.03.1885	Glasgow	Ireland	8–2	HI
25	21.03.1885	Kennington Oval	England	1–1	HI
26	23.03.1885	Wrexham	Wales	8–1	HI
27	20.03.1886	Belfast	Ireland	7–2	HI
28	31.03.1886	Glasgow	England	1–1	HI
29	10.04.1886	Glasgow	Wales	4–1	HI
30	19.02.1887	Glasgow	Ireland	4–1	HI
31	19.03.1887	Blackburn	England	3–2	HI
32	21.03.1887	Wrexham	Wales	2–0	HI
33	10.03.1888	Edinburgh	Wales	5–1	HI
34	17.03.1888	Glasgow	England	0–5	HI
35	24.03.1888	Belfast	Ireland	10–2	HI
36	09.03.1889	Glasgow	Ireland	7–0	HI
37	13.04.1889	Kennington l Oval	England	3–2	HI
38	15.04.1889	Wrexham	Wales	0–0	HI

Played 26 Won 22 Drew 2 Lost 4

Thanks to Jostein Nygård for the above information.

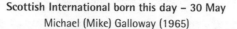

> **Scottish International born this day – 30 May**
> Michael (Mike) Galloway (1965)

> **Scottish Internationals born this day – 31 May**
> William Loney (1879); Stuart Robert Kennedy (1953)

— SALTIRE SEMINAR —

Defeat by Austria at Hampden in December 1950 ended Scotland's undefeated home run against foreign opposition – Austria (1933, 2–2); Germany (1936, 2–0); Czechoslovakia (1937, 5–0); Hungary (1938, 3–1); Belgium (1948, 2–0); France (1949, 2–0); Switzerland (1950, 3–1).

> **Scottish International born this day – 1 June**
> Henry Rennie (1873)

> **Scottish International born this day – 2 June**
> Thomas (Tommy) McLean (1947)

> **Scottish Internationals born this day – 3 June**
> Peter Somers (1878); George Elder Burley (1956)

> **Scottish International born this day – 4 June**
> Isaac Begbie (1868)

> **Scottish Internationals born this day – 5 June**
> Thomas Kelso (1882); James (Jim) Brogan (1944);
> Andrew (Andy) McLaren (1973)

— CALEDONIAN CHRONICLES —

SCOTLAND IN THE 1870s

Game No.	Date	Venue	Opponent	Score
1	30.11.1872	Glasgow	England	0–0
2	08.03.1873	Kennington Oval	England	2–4
3	07.03.1874	Glasgow	England	2–1
4	06.03.1875	Kennington Oval	England	2–2
5	04.03.1876	Glasgow	England	3–0
6	25.03.1876	Glasgow	Wales	4–0
7	03.03.1877	Kennington Oval	England	3–1
8	05.03.1877	Wrexham	Wales	2–0
9	02.03.1878	Glasgow	England	7–2
10	23.03.1878	Glasgow	Wales	9–0
11	05.04.1879	Kennington Oval	England	4–5
12	07.04.1879	Wrexham	Wales	3–0

Played 12 Won 8 Drew 1 Lost 3

Thanks to Jostein Nygård for the above information.

Scottish International born this day – 6 June
William McKrinnon (1859)

Scottish Internationals born this day – 7 June
Alexander Barbour (1862); James Howieson (1900);
John Miller (Ian) McColl (1927); Ian St John (1938);
Luigi (Lou) Macari (1949); Kevin Alastair Kyle (1981)

Scottish International born this day – 8 June
Archibald Baird (1919)

— BERSERKER BIOG – GRAHAM ALEXANDER —

Born in Coventry (England) on 10 October 1971, Graham qualified to play for Scotland via his Scottish-born father. Alexander was a latecomer to international football, following a career spent, for the most part, in the lower echelons of English football. He started his career with Scunthorpe United in 1989 before, in 1995, moving to Luton Town for four seasons. In the spring of 1999 Graham joined Preston North End and his first full season with the club coincided with them winning the Second Division Championship. Alexander became a regular in the side which continued to do well in the First Division. He spent his early years playing right midfield but it was only after a move to right-back that he found his strongest position. The first of his 30 caps was awarded for his appearance v Nigeria (17 April 2002) at Pittodrie Stadium, Aberdeen.

> **Scottish Internationals born this day – 9 June**
> Alexander Venters (1913); Henry (Harry) Yorston (1929)

> **Scottish Internationals born this day – 10 June**
> Joseph (Joe) McBride (1938);
> Andrew Stuart Murray (Stuart) McCall (1964)

— SALTIRE SEMINAR —

In 1951/52, Alan Morton, the Scotland and Rangers player, said, 'In Scotland today, there is only one international XI. Before the war, there were sufficient stars for several international teams.'

> **Scottish International born this day – 11 June**
> Andrew Baird (1866)

> **Scottish Internationals born this day – 12 June**
> David Haddow (1869); James Davidson Gibson (1901);
> Edward Hunter (Eddie) Turnbull (1923); David Narey (1956)

> **Scottish Internationals born this day – 13 June**
> John Connolly (1950); Alan David Hansen (1955)

> **Scottish International born this day – June 14**
> Alexander Thomson (1901)

— BERSERKER BIOG – CRAIG GORDON —

Edinburgh-born (31 December 1982) Craig Gordon is said by many of his fellow professionals to be the finest goalkeeper they have worked with.

He made his debut for Heart of Midlothian in 2002, aged 19, against Livingston, taking over from Tepi Moilanen a year later. After gaining a regular place, Craig never relinquished control of the number-one jersey. On 8 August 2007, Gordon joined Sunderland for a fee of £9m (£2m of which will be based on appearances), making him Britain's most expensive goalkeeper.

Gordon has been the Bank of Scotland Premier League Young Player of the Season and the Scottish Football Writers' Association Player of the Year. He made his international debut on 30 May 2004 (v Trinidad & Tobago), and, with 24 caps, he is now an established international player, regularly turning in magnificent performances for Scotland.

> **Scottish Internationals born this day – 15 June**
> John Rooney Gilmour (1901); Alan Bernard Brazil (1959)

> **Scottish Internationals born this day – 16 June**
> Robert Francis Dudgeon Ancell (1911);
> James Clews (Jimmy) Cowan (1926); John Grant (1931)

— A WEE JOKE —

Q. Why has Scotland never won the World Cup?
A. Because every time they get a corner, they put a fish and chip shop on it.

> **Scottish International born this day – 17 June**
> Robert 'The Sparrow' Brown (1858)

— BRITISH CHAMPIONSHIP RECORD —

Scotland have finished top of the British (Home International) Championship on 40 occasions compared to England's 53. Scotland have won the Championship outright on 24 occasions, nine times fewer than England's total.

YEAR	FIRST PLACE	SECOND PLACE	THIRD PLACE	FOURTH PLACE
1883/84 (1st)	Scotland	England	Wales	Ireland
1884/85 (2nd)	Scotland	England	Wales	Ireland
1885/86 (3rd)	Scotland & England	Wales	Ireland	
1886/87 (4th)	Scotland	England	Ireland	Wales
1887/88 (5th)	England	Scotland	Ireland	Wales
1888/89 (6th)	Scotland	England	Wales	Ireland
1889/90 (7th)	Scotland & England	Wales	Ireland	
1890/91 (8th)	England	Scotland	Ireland	Wales
1891/92 (9th)	England	Scotland	Ireland & Wales	
1892/93 (10th)	England	Scotland	Ireland	Wales
1893/94 (11th)	Scotland	England	Wales	Ireland
1894/95 (12th)	England	Wales & Scotland	Ireland	
1895/96 (13th)	Scotland	England	Wales	Ireland
1896/97 (14th)	Scotland	England	Ireland	Wales
1897/98 (15th)	England	Scotland	Ireland	Wales
1898/99 (16th)	England	Scotland	Ireland	Wales
1899/1900 (17th)	Scotland	Wales & England	Ireland	
1900/01 (18th)	England	Scotland	Ireland	Wales
1901/02 (19th)	Scotland	England	Ireland	Wales
1902/03 (20th)	England,	Ireland & Scotland	Wales	
1903/04 (21st)	England	Ireland	Wales & Scotland	
1904/05 (22nd)	England	Wales	Scotland & Ireland	
1905/06 (23rd)	England & Scotland	Wales	Ireland	
1906/07 (24th)	Wales	England	Scotland	Ireland
1907/08 (25th)	Scotland & England	Ireland	Wales	
1908/09 (26th)	England	Wales	Scotland	Ireland
1909/10 (27th)	Scotland	England & Ireland	Wales	
1910/11 (28th)	England	Scotland	Wales	Ireland

1911/12 (29th)	England & Scotland	Ireland	Wales	
1912/13 (30th)	England	Scotland & Wales	Ireland	
1913/14 (31st)	Ireland	Scotland	England	Wales
1914/19	No contest			
1919/20 (32nd)	Wales	Scotland & England	Ireland	
1920/21 (33rd)	Scotland	Wales & England	Ireland	
1921/22 (34th)	Scotland	England & Wales	Northern Ireland	
1922/23 (35th)	Scotland	England	Northern Ireland	Wales
1923/24 (36th)	Wales	Scotland	England	Northern Ireland
1924/25 (37th)	Scotland	England	Wales & Northern Ireland	
1925/26 (38th)	Scotland	Northern Ireland	Wales	England
1926/27 (39th)	Scotland & England	Northern Ireland & Wales		
1927/28 (40th)	Wales	Northern Ireland	Scotland	England
1928/29 (41st)	Scotland	England	Wales & Northern Ireland	
1929/30 (42nd)	England	Scotland	Northern Ireland	Wales
1930/31 (43rd)	Scotland & England	Wales	Northern Ireland	
1931/32 (44th)	England	Scotland	Northern Ireland	Wales
1932/33 (45th)	Wales	Scotland	England	Northern Ireland
1933/34 (46th)	Wales	England	Northern Ireland	Scotland
1934/35 (47th)	England & Scotland	Northern Ireland & Wales		
1935/36 (48th)	Scotland	England & Wales	Northern Ireland	
1936/37 (49th)	Wales	Scotland	England	Northern Ireland
1937/38 (50th)	England	Scotland & Northern Ireland		Wales
1938/39 (51st)	England, Scotland & Wales		Northern Ireland	
1939/46	No contest			
1946/47 (52nd)	England	Northern Ireland	Wales & Scotland	
1947/48 (53rd)	England	Wales	Northern Ireland	Scotland
1948/49 (54th)	Scotland	England	Wales	Northern Ireland
1949/50 (55th)	England	Scotland	Wales & Northern Ireland	
The 1950 competition also served as the World Cup qualification group 1				
1950/51 (56th)	Scotland	England	Wales	Northern Ireland
1951/52 (57th)	Wales & England	Scotland	Northern Ireland	
1952/53 (58th)	England & Scotland	Northern Ireland & Wales		
1953/54 (59th)	England	Scotland	Northern Ireland	Wales
The 1954 competition also served as the World Cup qualification group 3				
1954/55 (60th)	England	Scotland	Wales	Northern Ireland

Year				
1955/56 (61st)	England, Scotland, Wales & Northern Ireland			
1956/57 (62nd)	England	Scotland	Wales & Northern Ireland	
1957/58 (63rd)	England & Northern Ireland		Scotland & Wales	
1958/59 (64th)	Northern Ireland & England		Scotland	Wales
1959/60 (65th)	Scotland, England & Wales		Northern Ireland	
1960/61 (66th)	England	Wales	Scotland	Northern Ireland
1961/62 (67th)	Scotland	Wales	England	Northern Ireland
1962/63 (68th)	Scotland	England	Wales	Northern Ireland
1963/64 (69th)	England, Scotland & Northern Ireland		Wales	
1964/65 (70th)	England	Wales	Scotland	Northern Ireland
1965/66 (71st)	England	Northern Ireland	Scotland	Wales
1966/67 (72nd)	Scotland	England	Wales	Northern Ireland
The 1968 competition also served as the European Championship qualification group 8				
1967/68 (73rd)	England	Scotland	Wales & Northern Ireland	
1968/69 (74th)	England	Scotland	Northern Ireland	Wales
1969/70 (75th)	England, Scotland & Wales		Northern Ireland	
1970/71 (76th)	England	Northern Ireland	Wales	Scotland
1971/72 (77th)	England & Scotland	Northern Ireland	Wales	
1972/73 (78th)	England	Northern Ireland	Scotland	Wales
1973/74 (79th)	Scotland & England	Northern Ireland & Wales		
1974/75 (80th)	England	Scotland & Northern Ireland		Wales
1975/76 (81st)	Scotland	England	Wales	Northern Ireland
1976/77 (82nd)	Scotland	Wales	England	Northern Ireland
1977/78 (83rd)	England	Wales	Scotland	Northern Ireland
Goal Difference was added to the Championship Table to determine positions from 1979				
1978/79 (84th)	England	Wales	Scotland	Northern Ireland
1979/80 (85th)	Northern Ireland	England	Wales	Scotland
1980/81 (86th)	Scotland	Wales	England	Northern Ireland
Competition abandoned – unfinished and no winners				
1981/82 (87th)	England	Scotland	Wales	Northern Ireland
1982/83 (88th)	England	Scotland	Northern Ireland	Wales
1983/84 (89th)	Northern Ireland	Wales	England	Scotland

> **Scottish International born this day – 18 June**
> James (Jimmy) Mason (1919)

— SALTIRE SEMINAR —

When Scotland met England in a 'B' International at Roker Park, Sunderland, on 3 March 1954, it was the first time that a representative match in Britain had been played under floodlights.

> **Scottish Internationals born this day – 19 June**
> David Calderhead (1864); Robert (Rob) Neilson (1980)

> **Scottish Internationals born this day – 20 June**
> Peter Kerr (1891); Graham Leggatt (1934)

— SGIAN DUBH QUOTE —

A contract on a piece of paper saying you want to leave is like a piece of paper saying you want to leave.

John Collins (58 caps)

> **Scottish International born this day – 21 June**
> James Orr (1872)

> **Scottish Internationals born this day – 22 June**
> John Ferguson (1848); George Gillespie (1859); Leitch Keir (1861);
> Stephen Crainey (1981)

— BERSERKER BIOG – PAUL JAMES GALLACHER —

Born on 16 August 1979 in Glasgow, Paul signed for Norwich City on 2 June 2004, having moved from Dundee United on a free transfer.

He gained the first of his eight caps in the 0–1 defeat to Lithuania in a

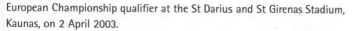

European Championship qualifier at the St Darius and St Girenas Stadium, Kaunas, on 2 April 2003.

Unable to shift Robert Green from the first team, Paul joined Gillingham on loan early in December 2004. He was recalled early on 27 December, but was loaned out again on 18 March 2005, joining former manager Paul Sturrock at Sheffield Wednesday for a month. This was extended until the end of that season.

Paul made his debut for Norwich on 15 April 2005 in a 1–0 defeat at Sheffield Wednesday, following an injury to Robert Green during the pre-match warm-up. He signed a new two-year contract on 12 June 2006.

Scottish International born this day – 23 June
William Semple Brown (Willie) Wallace (1940)

Scottish International born this day – 24 June
James Logan (1870)

— SALTIRE SEMINAR —

On the morning of Scotland's 1895 game with England at Goodison Park there was no sign of Dan Doyle, the Scottish skipper. The selectors had called up Bob Foyers (St Bernard's) at lunchtime. However, Dan arrived in time to claim his place, having spent the night with an old Everton team-mate (or so he said!).

Scottish Internationals born this day – 25 June
Paul Anthony Hegarty (1954); Cullum Iain Davidson (1976); Richard Daniel Hughes (1979); Scott Brown (1985)

Scottish Internationals born this day – 26 June
William Bowie (Willie) Campbell (1920); Gordon McQueen (1952)

— A WEE JOKE —

Just before England play Brazil, Ronaldo goes into the Brazilian changing room to find all his team-mates looking a bit glum.

'What's up?' he asks.

'Well, we're having trouble getting motivated for this game. We know it's important but it's only England. They're shite and we can't be bothered.'

Ronaldo looks at them and says, 'Well, I reckon I can beat these by myself; you lads go down the pub.'

So Ronaldo goes out to play England by himself and the rest of the Brazilian team go off for a few bevies.

After a couple of pints, they wonder how the game is going, so they get the landlord to put the teletext on. A big cheer goes up as the screen reads 'Brazil 1 – England 0 (Ronaldo 10 minutes).' He is beating England all by himself!

Anyway, a few more pints later and the game is forgotten until someone says, 'It must be full-time now; let's see how he got on.' They put the teletext on.

'Result from the stadium – Brazil 1 (Ronaldo 10 minutes) – England 1 (England have scored in the dying seconds of the game).'

The rest of the Brazilian team can't believe it; single-handed Ronaldo got a draw against England!! They rush back to the stadium to congratulate him. They find him in the dressing room, still in his gear, sat with his head in his hands.

He refuses to look at them. 'I've let you down, I've let you down.'

'Don't be daft! You got a draw against England, all by yourself. And they only scored at the very end!'

'No, No, I have, I've let you down ... I got sent off after 12 minutes.'

Scottish Internationals born this day – 27 June
Hugh McIntyre (1855); George Alexander Bowman (1872)

Scottish Internationals born this day – 28 June
John Bell Barker (1869); Andrew Clark Herd (1902);
Robert Inglis (Bobby) Campbell (1922)

— SALTIRE SEMINAR —

A trial match took place between Scotsmen playing in Scotland and the Scotsmen playing in England on 25 March 1896. In front of a crowd of 20,000, the ex-patriots won 2–1 at Ibrox. Following this event, trial games between 'Home' Scots and 'Anglo' Scots were played on a regular basis.

Scottish International born this day – 29 June
Andrew (Andy) Kerr (1931)

Scottish International born this day – 30 June
John Kelly (Dixie) Deans (1946)

— SGIAN DUBH QUOTE —

He's got a groin strain and he's been playing with it.
Alex McLeish (77 caps and Scotland manager)

Scottish International born this day – 1 July
Wilson Humphries (1928)

Scottish International born this day – 2 July
Thomas (Tommy) Gemmell (1930)

— SALTIRE SEMINAR —

For the Scotland v England game at Villa Park in 1899, the visitors refused to include the Villa star James Cowan after he had upset the selectors. Scotland missed Cowan as England scored seven lucky goals (five more than Scotland).

Scottish International born this day – 3 July
Michael Joseph (Mike) Cullen (1931)

Scottish International born this day – 4 July
Robert Gardner (1850)

— BERSERKER BIOG – RUSSELL ANDERSON —

Born in Aberdeen on 25 October 1978, Russell made his debut for Aberdeen in the Scottish Premier League in 1997. He joined the Dons from Dyce Juniors (his local senior team) in the summer of 1996 and went on to captain the side. He recently celebrated a decade with Aberdeen with a testimonial match against Everton, a game which attracted a crowd of 12,000. He is a fine defensive player and a solid and reliable centre-back; tall and blond, he became a real fans' favourite and amassed over 300 appearances for Aberdeen.

On 27 June 2007, Anderson joined Sunderland for a fee of £1m (he donated his £90,000 signing-on fee to Aberdeen's youth set-up).

Russell has played for the Scottish national side on 10 occasions and was both a Youth and Under-21 International. He has shown the same consistent form for both club and country over the last couple of seasons.

In November 2006, Russell won the Scottish Player of the Month award for the first time in his career.

Anderson made his Scotland debut in the Laugardalsvollur, Reykjavik, in the final minute of Scotland's 0–1 victory over Iceland.

Scottish Internationals born this day – 5 July
Gary Thomson Gillespie (1960); Derek John McInnes (1971)

Scottish International born this day – 6 July
John Lindsay (1862)

— SALTIRE SEMINAR —

In 1897, Jimmy Miller was knocked unconscious as he scored the goal that defeated England. Worried team-mate Neil Gibson asked, 'Are you all right?'

Coming round, Miller asked, 'Did I score?' Gibson assured him that he had indeed put Scotland a goal ahead, to which Jimmy responded, 'Then I'm all right.'

Tartan Army after a 1-0 victory at Wembley

Home International Championships 1895

Friendly v Argentina 1923

World Cup Spain 1982

World Cup Mexico 1986

Euro '96

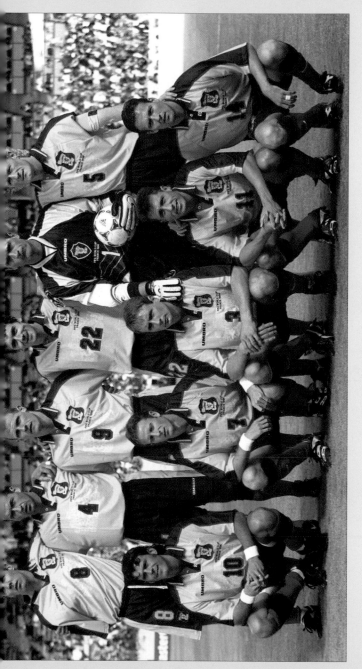

World Cup France 1998

Euro Qualifiers 2007

—— BERSERKER BIOG – CHRISTIAN EDWARD DAILLY ——

Born on 23 October 1973 in Dundee, Dailly is a versatile player in the backline or in the role of a defensive midfielder, but he has filled most outfield positions during his career. Unlike most modern footballers, the married father-of-four does not have an agent and negotiates deals on his own behalf.

Dailly was 16 when he played his first game for Dundee United, the youngest player ever to appear in the club's first team. He scored in his debut match against Alloa Athletic, having signed professional forms with the club on 2 August 1990. In fact, he scored in each of his first three games playing as a striker. In his first season, Dailly netted five times in 18 outings for the Terrors.

On 11 September 1990, Dailly made his Scotland Under-21 debut (aged 16) against Romania at Easter Road and so became the youngest player to appear for his country at that level. By the time Dailly was too old to continue playing at this level, he had received 34 caps, a world record for appearances at Under-21 level.

Christian won a Scottish Cup winners medal in 1994. It was his shot that rebounded off the post for Craig Brewster to score the only goal of the game against Rangers.

In 1996, at the end of his contract, he was offered huge salaries and packages to join Italian and Spanish clubs but moved to Derby County as it ensured that Dundee United would receive the £1m transfer fee and not lose him for free under the Bosman ruling.

Dailly joined the Rams in August 1996 for £500,000, with a further £500,000 payable, dependent on his international career (which was paid). In his debut English season, Christian missed just two games, with his three goals helping Derby to 12th place and six points clear of relegation in the Premier League.

In December 1998, Christian moved to Blackburn Rovers for £5.3m. In January 2001, he signed for West Ham United in a £1.75m deal. He made 12 appearances, helping the Hammers to 12th place in the Premiership. The following season, Dailly played every game as West Ham finished in 7th place. But 2002/03 proved to be a low point, as the East Londoners were relegated with the highest number of points since the 1995/96 change to 20 teams – 42.

In 2003–04, Dailly scored three times in 43 games as West Ham failed to win promotion. Injury prevented him from taking part in the majority of the Irons' promotion-winning 2004/05 season, although he was able to make cameo appearances in both play-off semi-final legs and the final.

Dailly appeared as a substitute for West Ham in their 2006 FA Cup Final defeat to Liverpool, coming on in the 77th minute. Had the Cockney boys won, Dailly would have become one of a few players to win both the Scottish Cup and FA Cup.

Dailly made his full international debut on 27 May 1997, aged 23, in a 1–0 defeat against Wales at the Rugby Park, Kilmarnock. His first international goal came in just his second match, and only four days after his first game for Scotland, when his early effort helped his country to a 3–2 victory over Malta in a friendly match at the Ta'Qali Stadium, Valetta.

— LEAGUE STATISTICS —

SEASON	CLUB	PLAYED	SCORED	DETAILS
1990/91	Dundee Utd	18	5	Debuts for Dundee Utd and Scotland U-21
1991/92	Dundee Utd	8	0	
1992/93	Dundee Utd	14	4	
1993/94	Dundee Utd	38	4	Wins Scottish Cup
1994/95	Dundee Utd	33	4	Relegated
1995/96	Dundee Utd	30	1	Promoted; joins Derby for £1m
1996/97	Derby	36	3	First Scotland cap and goal
1997/98	Derby	30	1	
1998/99	Derby	1	0	Joins Blackburn for £5.3m
1998/99	Blackburn	17	0	
1999/00	Blackburn	43	4	Relegated

2000/01	Blackburn	9	0	Joins West Ham for £1.75m
2000/01	West Ham	12	0	
2001/02	West Ham	38	0	
2002/03	West Ham	26	4	Relegated
2003/04	West Ham	43	3	
2004/05	West Ham	3	0	Promoted
2005/06	West Ham	21	0	FA Cup runners-up medal
2006/07	West Ham	17	0	
19 seasons	4 clubs	437	33	

— INTERNATIONAL STATISTICS —

YEAR	COUNTRY	PLAYED	SCORED	DETAILS
1997	Scotland	6	1	Debut v Wales; first goal v Malta
1998	Scotland	8	0	Plays all three games in 1998 World Cup
1999	Scotland	6	0	Scotland lose narrowly to England in Euro 2000 play-off
2000	Scotland	6	0	
2001	Scotland	4	0	
2002	Scotland	10	3	Captain for first time
2003	Scotland	10	0	
2004	Scotland	3	0	
2005	Scotland	7	1	
2006	Scotland	4	1	
11 years		65	6	

Scottish International born this day – 9 July
James Bowie (1888)

Scottish International born this day – 10 July
Andrew Watson (1857)

— SALTIRE SEMINAR —

The scorer of the first goal in the 1898 Scotland v England game was promised a bicycle as a reward. Aston Villa's George Wheldon won the bike, having opened the scoring for England after just three minutes. He rode it home to Birmingham after the match. The makers of the bike used the feat as publicity, nicknaming the cycle 'The Wheldon' and organised a race called 'England's Glory' from London to Birmingham in 1899. Unfortunately, there were only three starters and not one made it to the finish. Frenchman Jean Jacques Fouroux was initially awarded first prize but was eventfully disqualified when it was found out that his real name was Winthrope Tope and he had started out in Kettering! That was the first and last 'England's Glory' event.

Scottish International born this day – 11 July
Matthew Scott (1872)

Scottish International born this day – 12 July
Charles (Charlie) Fleming (1927)

— SGIAN DUBH QUOTE —

Some teams are so negative they could have been sponsored by Kodak.

Tommy Docherty (25 caps and former Scotland manager)

Scottish International born this day – 13 July
George Neil Farm (1924)

Scottish Internationals born this day – 14 July
Joseph (Joe) Dodds (1887); Duncan (Dunky) MacKay (1937);
Arthur Richard Albiston (1957); John Mark Colquhoun (1963)

— BERSERKER BIOG – GARY CALDWELL —

Born on 12 April 1982, in Stirling, Gary currently plays for Celtic at the centre of defence, but has played at right-back, as a defensive midfielder and man-marker at various points in his career.

Caldwell started his footballing life with Celtic Boys Club. At 16, he and his elder brother Steven signed for Newcastle United, but, unable to get a regular place in the first team, he went on loan to Darlington and Hibernian in 2001/02. This was followed the next season with further loan spells with Coventry City and Derby County. In the summer of 2003 Gary was given a free transfer to Hibs.

Caldwell won his first Scotland cap in 2002, under the reign of Berti Vogts (the German's first game as manager). He has now established himself as a national-squad member, if not first-team regular, but has played 25 times for his country, scoring twice.

Caldwell's international debut was not the happiest of occasions, the 5–0 defeat by France at the Stade de France on 27 March retrospectively set the tone of Vogts's tenure. It is a happy irony that probably the finest moment of his career so far also came against France when he scored the only goal of the game as Scotland defeated the World Cup runners-up 1–0 at Hampden Park on 7 October 2006 in a Euro 2008 qualifying match.

Scottish International born this day – 15 July
George W Wilson (1884)

Scottish International born this day – 16 July
Robert (Bobby) Evans (1927)

— SALTIRE SEMINAR —

Seven Rangers players were in the Scotland side that defeated Wales 5–2 in February 1900: Matt Dickie, Nicol Smith, David Crawford, Bobby Neill, Jacky Robertson, Bob Hamilton and Alex Smith.

Scottish International born this day – 17 July
Peter Barr Cormack (1946)

Scottish International born this day – 18 July
Jonathan Alan Gould (1968)

— SGIAN DUBH QUOTE —

The Scots are really knocking it about to some tune.
Alistair Alexander (media commentator)

— SALTIRE SEMINAR —

A few years after the turn of the 20th century, Jocky Simpson, an outside-right, who played for Falkirk, was selected to play for Scotland. However, his selection was withdrawn when the authorities found out that Jocky was in fact a Sassenach. Although both Simpson's parents were natives of Falkirk, their son had been born in Manchester. Jocky eventually joined Blackburn Rovers and made eight appearances for England, including the 1–1 draws against Scotland in 1911 and 1912 and was part of the English side that defeated Scotland 1–0 at Stamford Bridge in 1913.

Scottish International born this day – 19 July
William Longair (1870)

— BERSERKER BIOG – KRIS BOYD —

Born in Irvine, Ayrshire, on 18 August 1983, Boyd started his football career with Kilmarnock, making his debut for the club v Celtic in the final game of the 2000/01 season. The next term, following the departure of Ally McCoist and Christophe Cocard, Boyd took his chance to claim a place in the first team, and he scored five goals during the Killies' Scottish Premiership campaign.

During the 2002/03 season, Kris netted a dozen times and won the Kilmarnock Young Player of the Year award. Over the same period he became a regular in the Scotland Under-21 team. The following season, he scored 15 goals for Kilmarnock.

In September 2004, having hit all five of Kilmarnock's goals against Dundee United in the Killies' 5–2 victory, Boyd equalled the record for the highest number of goals scored in a single game.

It was announced on 22 December 2005 that Kris would sign for Rangers in the January transfer window. Boyd officially joined the Gers on 1 January 2006. In a generous gesture, he donated half of his £40,000 signing-on fee, which Kilmarnock were obliged to pay him under the terms of his contract, to help pay for the youth set-up which benefited him as a young player.

Kris played his first game for Rangers on 7 January 2006 against Peterhead in the Scottish Cup third round; he scored a hat-trick in his side's 5–0 win. Boyd went on to hit a score of goals in 17 appearances for his new club during the second half of the season. As such, he became the first player to finish top scorer at two clubs in one season, having scored 17 goals for Kilmarnock prior to his move to Ibrox.

Kris made his full international debut on 11 May 2006, scoring twice in the Kobe Wing Stadium, Kobe, during a 5–1 win over Bulgaria in the Kirin Cup in Japan. Boyd extended his fine international form into the European Championship qualifying competition, scoring two goals in Scotland's opening match against the Faroe Islands in September 2006. In his 10 appearances in a Scottish shirt, Boyd has scored six goals.

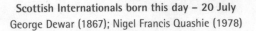

Scottish Internationals born this day – 20 July
George Dewar (1867); Nigel Francis Quashie (1978)

Scottish Internationals born this day – 21 July
John Evens Wright (Jackie) Sinclair (1943); Gary Teale (1978)

Scottish International born this day – 22 July
James Dunlop (1869)

Scottish Internationals born this day – 23 July
Kenneth Anderson (1875); Gladstone Hamilton (1879);
Hugh Thomas Kelly (1923)

Scottish International born this day – 24 July
James (Jim) Leighton (1958)

— SALTIRE SEMINAR —

During 1912 the Scottish Football Association made a request for Sunderland to release Charlie Buchan if he was selected for the next international. The Roker Park management agreed, knowing that Buchan's parents were both Aberdonians, but that he was, in fact, born in Woolwich, London. Buchan, of course, went on to represent England and be recognised as one of the best players of his era.

Scottish Internationals born this day – 25 July
Donald McKinlay (1891); Harry Haddock (1925); Darren Jackson (1966)

Scottish International born this day – 26 July
James Wilson (1866)

— SGIAN DUBH QUOTE —

Our keeper only had one save to make but we lost 4–0.
Craig Brown (former Scotland manager)

Scottish International born this day – 27 July
John Campbell Baird (1856)

Scottish International born this day – 28 July
Thomas Wylie (1872)

— SALTIRE SEMINAR —

In 1913 Scotland met the Irish in Ireland for the second successive year to help the Irish FA's financial situation.

Scottish Internationals born this day – 29 July
David Morton Steele (1894); John Eric (Eric) Smith (1934)

— BERSERKER BIOG – STEPHEN MCMANUS —

A product of Celtic's youth academy, McManus, a tall, left-sided defender, made his first-team debut under Martin O'Neill during the 2003/04 season.

McManus was born in Lanark on 10 September 1982 and gained Scottish Under-18 honours. In 2005/06 Steve cemented his place in the Celtic first team. He played in 42 games, scoring a useful eight goals but collecting a less than helpful 10 yellow cards in the process. For all this, his ability to play in a variety of positions across the backline is a valuable asset for both Celtic and Scotland.

McManus was made skipper for the first League game of the 2006/07 season in the match against Kilmarnock (regular club captain Neil Lennon having been suspended). After this, he deputised as Celtic's vice-captain throughout the 2006/07 season.

On 31 July 2007, McManus was officially announced as the captain of Celtic as he signed a new four-year contract. He said, 'To be given the captaincy of Celtic is a tremendous honour. It is undoubtedly one of the highlights of my career so far.'

Steve made his full international debut on 11 Oct 2006 at the Olympic Stadium, Kiev, in Scotland's 2–0 defeat at the hands of Ukraine and at the time of writing has acquired six caps.

Scottish International born this day – 30 July
Archibald Renwick (Archie) Macaulay (1915)

Scottish Internationals born this day – 31 July
Robert McKinnon (1966); Derek Ferguson (1967)

Scottish International born this day – 1 August
Henry McNeil (1850)

— BALLY RAMMY – THE FIRST WEMBLEY WIZARDS —

Perhaps the most celebrated international game Scotland have ever played was something of a disaster for England; the immortal Wembley Wizards on 31 March 1928 destroyed the home side 1–5 in the driving rain. Alex James and the rest of the Scottish side totally outplayed England. Only West Ham goalkeeper Ted Hufton's magnificent display prevented a more profound defeat. As it was, the second England v Scotland game at Wembley concluded as the most complete destruction inflicted on an English side in the history of the game and nothing like it would be seen again until Hungary came to call in 1953.

When the 1927/28 season started, Scotland were in a position to boost a magnificent post-war record; their 24 games since 1919 had produced 17 wins, three draws and four defeats.

In many ways, Scotland's magnificent destruction of England in 1928 was the summit of a great era, but encounters with Wales and Ireland in the first part of the season weren't memorable. Scotland were two goals ahead of the Welsh before 15 minutes had been played, but a dragon-like resurgence from the determined Druids took the shine off the day for the Scots and, although their centre-half Jimmy Gibson performed well, Wales managed a 2–2 draw.

As a consequence, four changes were made to the Scottish team initially chosen to play the Irish. Prolific scorer Jimmy McGrory was the only debutant and he was to have an exasperating initiation. Scotland completely dominated the play, but the Irish goalkeeper, Elisha Scott, had an outstanding game and somehow Scotland were defeated 1–0 by a goal from Chambers scored after 10 minutes, following Allan McClory making a mess of a cross.

Coming to Wembley, the Scots were unusually pessimistic. Unlike the all-tartan team of 1925, only three 'Home-Scots' faced England in 1928. Experienced men like John Hutton, Billy McStay and David Meiklejohn were left out of the Scottish line-up. Andy Cunningham and Rob McPhail were overlooked, and Hughie Gallacher was preferred over Jim McGrory even though he had just completed a two-month suspension. Tommy Law and 'Tiny' Bradshaw were given their international debuts and Alex James won his second cap. It was a relatively inexperienced team, but the game would decide who finished last in the British Championship, so the Scots, although obviously not wanting to be defeated by England, had less to lose than in previous years and as such took the opportunity to experiment.

The day before the match, the Scottish captain Jim McMullan reviewed Scotland's smallest-ever forward line; only Alex Jackson stood over 5ft 6in. Jim told them, 'Pray for rain.'

If they did offer up an entreaty, it was successful, as the rain on the day of the match made Wembley a greasy surface to play on, which was perfect for the diminutive Scottish strikers, with their relatively low centres of gravity. On a number of occasions when in possession, the visitors gave the impression that the ball was working its way along an invisible line strung between the Scottish players; at times, it was moving from one end of the pitch to the other without an English player touching it.

It's probably the case that the English selectors could not have named a stronger side and that it was the sheer class of the Scottish side that won the day. J.H. Freeman in the *Daily Mail* pulled no punches in his summation of events: 'Let us be quite frank and admit that – temporarily at any rate – we have lost the art of breeding individual players of superlative merit or the genius for team-building – or both ... in all the annals of international football I do not think there is a parallel to this match. The inferiority of the England side was so marked that the confusion and bewilderment of the individual players, against the science and skill and pace of Scotland's dazzling team, became positively ludicrous.'

However, things did not look good for the visitors when England hit a Scottish post in the first minute. But the ball rebounded to McMullan, who, reacting like lightning, set up a move between James and Dunn that got the ball to Morton who swiftly clipped over a centre for Jackson to head Scotland into the lead. Just before the interval, Jackson made it 2–0.

Scotland dominated the second half. James hit the bar and, although Hammer Ted Hufton made several fine saves, Jackson eventually made it 3–0.

The hat-trick by winger Alex Jackson, who tormented the English left-back Herbert Jones, highlighted the weakness of the English defence and, according to Freeman, 'Right-half Edwards worked hard and at times effectively ... But of what avail were the puny efforts of one man against a team of giants?'

The prolific goalscorer 'Dixie' Dean was cut out of the game by an efficient Scottish defence, the only near-effective English forward being inside-right Bob Kelly, although he was constantly berated by the crowd for holding on to the ball, but Freeman was on his side, commenting, 'No wonder. While he had the ball there was just a chance of something happening; when he parted with it the movement just fizzled out.'

The Scottish strike force was almost faultless; the wingers Morton and Jackson were magnificent as a pair, while the splendour of Gallacher never shone brighter. James and Jimmy Dunn went past England's halves as if they were ghosts. For Freeman, 'In one movement – and it was typical – the ball went 11 times to a Scottish player without touching an English boot or head ... Scotland's whole team played with a dominant mastery that was made to appear sheer effrontery.'

Gallacher set up Scotland's fourth for James and the handful was completed with a second from the Preston player.

Bob Kelly's goal, from a free-kick, just before the end of the game, did little to placate the disappointment of the 80,868 crowd, but most remained to clap Hufton from the field; he had thwarted every Scottish forward more than once. Hughie Gallacher, years later, was to claim that, if it had not have been for the bravery and skill of England's 'Tiger', Scotland would have got to double figures. Such was the penetrative power of the Caledonian forwards, on many occasions Hufton was obliged to hold off two or three tartan raiders single-handed.

There was no real defect in Scotland's defence where Bradshaw had pinned 'Dixie' Dean down. 'Tiny' was a 'footballing' centre-half, but he had a penchant for dribbling his way out of trouble. The Wembley game was to be his only cap; ironically, the 'Wembley Wizards' came together for just that one memorable afternoon in March 1928.

Scottish skipper Jim McMullan later commented that England's wing-halves had allowed Scotland's inside players too much room. Whatever the reason for the eventual massacre, the memory of this great victory would lie sweetly in Scottish hearts for many years to come.

SCOTLAND	CAPS	CLUB	GOALS	ENGLAND	CLUB	GOALS
John Harkness	3	Queen's Park		Arthur Edward Hufton	West Ham United	
James Nelson	3	Cardiff City		Frederick Roy Goodall (Captain)	Huddersfield Town	
Thomas Law	1	Chelsea		Herbert Jones	Blackburn Rovers	
James Gibson	6	Aston Villa		Willis Edwards	Leeds United	
Thomas Bradshaw	1	Bury		Thomas Wilson	Huddersfield Town	
James McMullan (Captain)	13	Manchester City		Henry Healless	Blackburn Rovers	
Alex Jackson	10	Huddersfield Town	2,44,65	Joseph Harold Anthony Hulme	Arsenal	
James Dunn	5	Hibernian		Robert F.Kelly	Huddersfield Town	89
Hugh Gallacher	12	Newcastle United		William Ralph (Dixie) Dean	Everton	
Alex James	2	Preston North End	67,85	Joseph Bradford	Huddersfield Town	
Alan Morton	19	Rangers		William Henry Smith		

Referee: William Bell (Scotland)

Scottish Internationals born this day – 2 August
Francis Barrett (1872); Alexander Hershaw (Alex) Parker (1935)

Scottish International born this day – 3 August
Maurice Malpas (1962)

— SGIAN DUBH QUOTE —

I refereed Croatia against Bosnia at a time when they were at war with each other and it was an easier game to handle than the Old Firm.

Hugh Dallas (Scottish referee)

Scottish Internationals born this day – 4 August
John Wark (1957); Robert Connor (1960)

Scottish International born this day – 5 August
William Ker (1850)

— SALTIRE SEMINAR —

Canadian-born goalkeeper Joe Kennaway had played for Canada (against USA in 1928) before appearing for Scotland in 1934. He'd also turned out for the USA (against Canada in 1930). Kennaway is the only Scottish International to have played for two other countries and one of the very few footballers to have been capped by three different nations.

Scottish International born this day – 6 August
Erich Peter Schaedler (1949)

— BERSERKER BIOG – JAMES MCFADDEN —

Born 14 April 1983 in Springburn, Glasgow, McFadden became part of the Motherwell youth system as a youngster and made his first-team debut when he was just 17.

It was during the Scottish Premiership season of 2002/03 that James scored 19 goals from 34 starts and won the Scottish Young Player of the Year award. But his tally of 15 yellow cards and one red was not so impressive.

McFadden gained his first Scotland cap at Hong Kong Stadium, Hong

Kong, aged 19 on a Far East Tour playing in the Reunification Cup against South Africa and assisted in the 2–0 victory.

Jimmy's performances led to a regular place in the Scotland squad and he scored his first international goal at Hampden Park against the Faroe Islands in the Euro 2004 qualifying match of 6 September 2003 (the home side won 3–1). He now has 32 caps and 10 international goals to his credit.

In 2003, McFadden moved to Everton for a fee of £1.25m, and on 1 January 2005 he netted his first goal for the Toffees in their 5–2 victory at White Hart Lane. A week later, James scored his second goal in an FA Cup third-round tie against Plymouth.

Throughout 2006, McFadden (also known as Mac or Faddy to his Everton and Scottish team-mates) improved steadily and has scored some fine goals against the likes of Manchester United, Chelsea, Fulham, Aston Villa and Middlesbrough.

Scottish International born this day – 7 August
Paul Lambert (1969)

— BARRY RAMMY – AVEC LES BLEUS —

Scotland has played France 14 times: they have won seven and lost seven. One of the most important and impressive of Scotland's victories over their erstwhile 'Auld Alliance Ami' was the UEFA European Championship qualifier of 7 October 2006 at Hampden Park in front of 50,406 hopeful supporters. The last meeting between the two nations, in March 2002, ended in a 5–0 thrashing for the Scots in Paris, as the Berti Vogts era started as it was doomed to progress.

Before the game, Walter Smith, the Scottish manager, had asked the Tartan Army to be reasonable about Scotland's chances but the crowd at Hampden were looking forward to an evening to remember, many of them having memories of or having heard stories of their last win over 'Les Bleus' in Glasgow in 1989 when a brace from Maurice Johnston had helped Scotland to a notable victory.

James McFadden was selected ahead of Kris Boyd and Garry O'Connor got the nod as the lone forward (Kenny Miller had been suspended). Barry

Ferguson, who had been out of the Scottish side since March due to injury, was given the captain's armband by Smith.

Raymond Domenech, the French head coach, named Patrick Vieira and Willy Sagnol in his starting XI after both had been passed fit. However, the injured William Gallas was replaced by former Rangers defender Jean-Alain Boumsong, while Manchester United star Louis Saha was on the bench.

The fans were well behind Scotland as the side broke up the pitch just seconds into the game; Lee McCulloch sent a tantalising ball into the box but, frustratingly, there was not a Scotsman in sight to meet the cross and Gregory Coupet comfortably dealt with the threat.

Scotland got another opportunity when McFadden stole the ball from Lilian Thuram on the by-line only to witness his drive ricochet off the body of team-mate Paul Hartley.

France were awarded a free-kick on the edge of the box after Thierry Henry was floored by Caldwell; however, a curling shot from the legendary Frenchman clattered the post.

Scotland were once more under pressure when France won another free-kick in a perilous area. David Weir had fouled Henry but, this time, the forward's shot was easily dealt with by Craig Gordon.

France looked to have scored when Patrick Vieira met Franck Ribery's free-kick and headed into the Scottish net from less than 20 feet out, but the offside flag was raised before Vieira made contact.

The World Cup finalists were making the better chances for themselves; Florent Malouda delivered a subtle pass into the stride of Sagnol on the right wing but his effort dropped across the face of goal and wide.

An acrobatic overhead kick by David Trezeguet went trickling over the line but the flag flew up as he made contact; he was clearly offside.

In the 29th minute McFadden was the first player to be booked, the offending challenge on Boumsong. Three minutes later, the Everton striker Andy McCulloch received a yellow card as his reward for taking a kick at Vieira.

Scotland might have grabbed the lead before half-time after Caldwell's head met Hartley's corner from close range. Regrettably, the ball seemed to be directed into Coupet's arms.

At the start of the second 45 minutes, Scotland went for the French with a purpose. McFadden skipped round two defenders to pick up a long ball from Darren Fletcher; unfortunately he screwed the shot wide of the post.

A collision between Henry and Gordon in the box concluded with the Scottish keeper coming off second best, although he was able to carry on after treatment.

With a little less than 60 minutes played, Scotland made their first change, McCulloch was replaced by Gary Teale, his team-mate from Wigan. Shortly after that, the French brought on Louis Saha to replace Trezeguet.

It looked to be a game that was running out to a well-played draw until the French were rocked in the 67th minute. An in-swinging corner from Hartley landed at the feet of Caldwell; a dozen yards out, he took his chance well, poking his second international goal low into the back of the French rigging. Hampden Park erupted.

Moments later, Christian Dailly was booked for time-wasting (meaning he missed the next qualifier against the Ukraine).

Scotland could have made it 2–0 when Ferguson drifted the ball into the path of Hartley in front of goal. However, Vieira intercepted and cleared the French lines before Hartley could make contact.

Substitute O'Connor hit a long-range strike in the final minute, but the French replied with an attack of their own and the home side were only saved by a superb block by Gordon from a fine effort by Sagnol.

In the last analysis Caldwell's goal was to be enough for Smith's warriors to tighten their grip on pole position in Group B of the European Championship and gave Scottish hopes of qualifying for the European finals a massive boost.

The Celtic man became an instant hero as Scotland brought one of the finest teams on earth to their knees in defeat. Maximum points from their opening two qualifiers against the Faroe Islands and Lithuania the previous month seemed to indicate that the Scotland team had progressed in leaps and bounds in terms of self-belief and confidence. They sat atop Group B, ahead of France on goal difference.

France coach – Raymond Domenech
Scotland manager – Walter Smith

SCOTLAND	CLUB	CAPS	GOALS	FRANCE
Craig Gordon	Heart of Midlothian	18		Grégory Coupet
Christian Dailly	West Ham United	63		Willy Sagnol
Graham Alexander	Preston North End	24		Lilian Thuram
Steven Pressley	Heart of Midlothian	31		Jean-Alain Boumsong
David Weir *	Everton	50		Eric Abidal
Barry Ferguson (Captain)	Rangers	34		Claude Makelele
Darren Fletcher	Manchester United	26		Patrick Vieira (Captain)
Gary Caldwell	Celtic	22	67	Franck Ribery (Sylvain Wiltord, 73)
James McFadden (O'Connor, 71)	Everton	30		Thierry Henry
Paul Hartley	Heart of Midlothian	10		Florent Malouda
Lee McCulloch (Teale, 57)	Wigan Athletic	8		David Trezeguet (Louis Saha, 61)
Garry O'Connor (McFadden, 71)	FK Lokomotiv Moskva	8		Louis Saha (David Trezeguet, 61)
Gary Teale (McCulloch, 57)	Wigan Athletic	5		

Referee – Massimo Busacca (Switzerland)

*David Weir is the 25th player to reach 50 caps for Scotland.

Scottish Internationals born this day – 8 August
William Alexander (Willie) Woodburn (1919);
William Yates (Willie) Redpath (1922); Thomas (Tommy) Ring (1930)

— SGIAN DUBH QUOTE —

Faroes 1, Fairies 1.
Headline in two Scottish newspapers after Scotland's draw with the northerly minnows in a Euro 2000 qualifier

---

Scottish Internationals born this day – 9 August
Andrew McIntyre (1855); William Duncan Cowan (1896);
Paul Gallagher (1984)

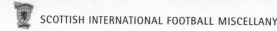

— SALTIRE SEMINAR —

Straight after World War I, referees in British Championship games were neutral, but one linesman from each of the opposing countries was used in any given match. As such, Burslem referee Mr J. Mason officiated at the Wales v Scotland game in Cardiff during 1920, while the Scottish FA president Mr T. White ran the line.

Scottish International born this day – 10 August
Joseph Cassidy (1896)

— BERSERKER BIOG – ROBBIE NEILSON —

Born 19 June 1980, in Paisley, Heart of Midlothian right-back Neilson was originally a product of Rangers Boys Club system, but he joined Hearts Youth Academy at 16, feeling the move would offer him a greater opportunity of first-team football, as few of Robbie's contemporaries at Rangers have established themselves at Ibrox, where the high expectations of supporters have led to a succession of highly paid foreign signings being preferred to local talent.

Robbie had loan spells at Cowdenbeath (1999/2000) and Queen of the South (2002/03) before making a first-team place his own at Tynecastle.

Although not the speediest of defenders and lacking more subtle footballing skills, Neilson has a good positional awareness and is well known for his long throw-ins, which can be just as good as a corner from halfway inside the opponents' half.

Neilson has represented his country at Under-21 level but the pinnacle of his career to date is probably his game-winner in Hearts' 2–1 win at St Jakob-Park against FC Basel in the 2004/05 UEFA Cup, surprisingly his first goal in any competition for the club.

Robbie won his first Scotland cap in the 2–0 defeat to Ukraine on 11 October 2006, and has Scottish Cup (2005/06) and Scottish League Challenge Cup (2002/03) medals.

Scottish Internationals born this day – 11 August
Andrew Beattie (1913); Robert William Fleck (1965);
Neil McCann (1974)

— SALTIRE SEMINAR —

John McPherson, who was a Scottish International between 1879 and 1885, once invited the English reporter Jim Catton to see the ground where the first international took place. Catton could see nothing that bore much of a resemblance to a football field and asked where he should be looking. McPherson told him, 'Why there, mon ... That's Bannockburn!'

Scottish International born this day – 12 August
John Smith (1855)

— SALTIRE SEMINAR —

Scotland made an innovative two-month tour of Canada and the United States during the summer of 1921. The 'Scottish Soccerites', as they were called by the American media, were victorious in their 19 games in Canada, scoring 85 goals, the majority of which were claimed by Andy Wilson. A 1–0 win in Montreal was the closest the tourists came to failing to win. For the half-dozen matches in the USA, Scotland were billed as 'Third Lanark'.

Following a close game in New York, Scotland scored the winner two minutes from time. Scotland arrived at Fall River for the 25th and last game of their expedition with a perfect record. The team had been guaranteed 75 per cent of the receipts with a minimum of $1,000 for their final match. Against the local team, a tired Scotland managed a 2–2 draw in front of 3,682 people. Crowds of this size made the tour a financial success. On their return, the tour organiser, Glasgow sportswriter Robert Connell, said, 'Our trip, the first of its kind ever attempted, will do more to boost this great game than anything else I can conceive of.'

— MANAGERS —

From 1872 to 1954 the Scotland national team was appointed by an SFA selection committee.

Manager	Scotland career	Played	Won	Drawn	Lost
Selection committee	1872–1954 1954–1958	254	148	48	58
Andy Beattie	1954	6	2	1	3
Dawson Walker*	1958	6	1	2	3
Matt Busby	1958	2	1	1	0
Andy Beattie	1959–1960	11	4	3	4
Ian McColl	1960–1965	28	17	3	8
Jock Stein	1965–1966	7	3	1	3
John Prentice	1966	4	0	1	3
Malcolm MacDonald	1966–1967	2	1	1	0
Bobby Brown	1967–1971	28	9	8	11
Tommy Docherty	1971–1972	12	7	2	3
Willie Ormond	1973–1977	38	18	8	12
Ally MacLeod	1977–1978	17	7	5	5
Jock Stein	1978–1985	61	26	12	23
Alex Ferguson	1985–1986	10	3	4	3
Andy Roxburgh	1986–1993	62	23	19	20
Craig Brown	1993–2002	70	32	18	20
Berti Vogts	2002–2004	30	7	7	16
Tommy Burns**	2004	1	0	0	1
Walter Smith	2004–2007	16	7	5	4
Alex McLeish	2007–Present	5	5	0	1
Totals		**669**	**319**	**149**	**201**

*Matt Busby was officially the Scotland Manager, but Dawson Walker, the team trainer, was left in charge of the players in February 1956 after the Munich air disaster in which Busby was seriously injured.

**Tommy Burns was caretaker manager following the departure of Berti Vogts. All Scotland's managers except Berti Vogts (who is German) were born in Scotland.

Scottish International born this day – 13 August
William MacKinnon (1850)

Scottish International born this day – 14 August
Donald Colman (1878)

— SGIAN DUBH QUOTE —

Ian Durrant has grown both physically and metaphorically in the close season.

Jock Wallace (former Rangers manager)

Scottish International born this day – 15 August
John McPherson (1867)

— SALTIRE SEMINAR —

In February 1924, Scotland met Wales at Ninian Park, Cardiff. Both captains, Jimmy Blair (Scotland) and Charlie Keenor (Wales), ran out on their home club ground. Scotland had Welsh-Scots in both full-back positions. Blair was partnered by 'the ferro-concrete full-back', hefty Jock Marshall, who was still thought to be of international quality, even though he was playing for non-League club Llanelli.

Scottish Internationals born this day – 16 August
Leslie Hamilton Johnston (1920);
Robert Carmichael (Bobby) Mitchell (1924); Paul Gallacher (1979)

— SGIAN DUBH QUOTE —

It's the carrot at the end of the rainbow.

Danny McGrain (62 caps)

Scottish Internationals born this day – 17 August
James Adams (1864); Robert (Bobby) Murdoch (1944)

— BERSERKER BIOG – STEVEN JOHN PRESSLEY —

Pressley first saw the light of day on 11 October 1973 in Elgin, Moray, and, given his surname, it is unsurprising that he is often known as Elvis.

He started his career at Rangers as a youngster and was seen by the media as 'the new Richard Gough'. But Pressley struggled to establish himself as a regular and was transferred to Coventry City during 1994 for a fee of £630,000. However, after just one year, following problems with his form and disciplinary record, he returned to Scotland. Dundee United paid £750,000 for his services, but he helped the Terrors to third place in the League in 1996–97.

Pressley's organisational skills and intelligent playing style were the bait that caused Hearts to sign him on a Bosman free transfer in 1998.

Hearts finished second in the League in 2005/06, third on three occasions and reached the Scottish and League Cup semi-finals, with Pressley being hugely influential on the pitch. He was regarded by Hearts fans as the mainstay of the club and acted as an advocate for the playing squad in response to the series of controversies affecting Hearts under the ownership of Vladimir Romanov.

Steve's enrolment into the Hearts Hall of Fame highlights the status which he enjoyed at Tynecastle. Pressley led the club in their triumphant Scottish Cup run of 2006.

On 9 December 2006, it was confirmed that Pressley and Hearts had parted company following the latest run-in with Romanov. By the end of the month Steven Pressley had been signed as a free agent by Celtic.

Pressley has been capped 32 times since his debut on 29 March 2000 against France (a 0–2 defeat at Hampden Park) and has captained the national side once.

Steven's appearance against Lithuania in the 2–1 victory in the St Darius and St Girenas Stadium, Kaunas, on 6 September 2006 saw him surpass Bobby Walker's record as Hearts' most capped Scottish player, a record which has stood for 91 years. But Pressley also became the first Scottish player to be sent off in Scotland's Euro 2008 qualifying campaign; he got his marching orders in the away game against Ukraine on 11 October 2006, Scotland's first defeat of the campaign. This game fell on Pressley's 33rd birthday.

Scottish Internationals born this day – 18 August
Finlay Ballantyne Speedie (1880); Mark James Burchill (1980);
Kris Boyd (1983): John Kennedy (1983)

— SALTIRE SEMINAR —

Scotland, with a team of 'home' Scots, defeated England in 1925. But seven of the side joined English clubs: Willie Harper (£4,500 to Arsenal), Phil McCloy (£3,000 to Manchester City), Davie Morris (£4,700 to Preston), Jimmy McMullan (£4,700 to Manchester City), Alex Jackson (£5,000 to Huddersfield), Willie Russell (£3,650 to Preston) and Hughie Gallacher (£6,500 to Newcastle).

Scottish International born this day – 19 August
Matthew Dickie (1873)

— BERSERKER BIOG – DAVID GILLESPIE WEIR —

Born in Falkirk on 10 May 1970, as a teenager, Weir trained with the Celtic youth sides. Out of character with most players of his calibre, Weir put his professional career on hold to play college soccer in the USA at the University of Evansville from 1988 to 1991. Dave did well enough with the Evansville defence to be named as an NCAA All-American in 1990.

In 1992 Weir signed for Scottish First Division side Falkirk. He was to play 150 games for the Bairns. In 1996 he moved to Hearts in the Scottish Premier League and won a Scottish Cup winners medal in 1998. David left Tynecastle for Goodison in 1999, but was back in Scotland with Rangers from 16 January 2007 after Everton released him from his contract early.

Weir was awarded his first cap in 1997, a 0–1 defeat to Wales at Rugby Park, Kilmarnock, on 27 May 1997. He later retired from international football after he was criticised by the then Scotland manager Berti Vogts. However, he returned to the Scottish ranks after Walter Smith, his former manager at Everton, was appointed Scotland's new manager in December

2004. Dave has been initiated into the Scotland Football Hall of Fame, having won his 50th Scotland cap against Lithuania on 6 September 2006; he captained his country to a 2–1 win that day.

On 16 January 2007, Weir signed for Rangers, the side he has supported since his boyhood, on an initial six-month deal, reuniting him with his former manager Walter Smith. He later secured a one-year contract and in April 2007 it was revealed that he would stay with Rangers for the 2007/08 season.

Weir is a member of the management committee of the Professional Footballers Association. He has now made 56 appearances for his country and scored one goal.

Scottish Internationals born this day – 20 August
William Hall Berry (1867); Ronald (Ron) McKinnon (1940);
Robert (Bobby) Lennox (1943)

— A WEE JOKE —

Q. What do you get if you see an England fan buried up to his neck in sand?
A. More sand.

Scottish Internationals born this day – 21 August
James (Jim) Scott (1940); David Hopkin (1970);
Paul Simon Ritchie (1975)

— SALTIRE SEMINAR —

During the 1920s, Scotland's record in international games was second to none. They had amassed 24 wins and five draws in 34 matches. This included a 747-minute period (February 1925 to April 1927) wherein Scotland did not concede a goal and scored 20.

Scottish International born this day – 22 August
David Murray McPherson (1872)

— SGIAN DUBH QUOTE —

They had a dozen corners, maybe 12 – I'm guessing.

Craig Brown (former Scotland manager)

Scottish Internationals born this day – 23 August
James Findlay (Jimmy) Stephen (1922); Paul Wilson (1950)

— BERSERKER BIOG – GARY TEALE —

Teale won his first cap on 11 May 2006 in Scotland's 5–1 defeat of Bulgaria at the Kobe Wing Stadium, Kobe, Japan, in the Kirin Cup. He has now represented his country on nine occasions to add to his half-dozen Under-21 caps with Clydebank (where he had been a trainee) and Ayr United, playing for the former from 1996 to 1998, and at Somerset Park until 2001. Teale made over 100 appearances for his first two clubs, scoring 18 times.

Born in Glasgow on 21 July 1978, Gary is a promising attacking midfield talent. He moved south to Wigan Athletic in 2001 for a fee of £200,000. Making 31 starts in his first season, scoring twice, Teale took a key role in the club's rise to the Premiership. He is a player with a superb sense of positioning and electrifying pace. His contract with the Latics was renewed for two years in 2005.

Gary didn't score during the 2005/06 season, but he was once more a vital member of the Wigan team, playing 33 games.

On 11 January 2007, Teale moved to Derby County for a fee of £600,000. Although he showed promise during his initial period at Pride Park, his form dipped, resulting in his being second choice to Craig Fagan for the latter part of the 2006/07 season.

Scottish Internationals born this day – 24 August
Alexander Iain (Iain) Munro (1951); Barry Nicholson (1978)

Scottish International born this day – 25 August
Alexander McMahon (1870)

— SALTIRE SEMINAR —

Scotland undertook a tour of Canada in 1927. They achieved their seventh victory in eight games when they defeated a touring Austrian side, Hookalls, 4–1, on 19 June. But the game in Winnipeg was tarnished by violence. In Toronto, on 11 July, Scotland achieved a 3–0 win against the Ulster United National League team. Probably the biggest surprise of the tour came when Toronto beat a Scottish XI 3–2. However, the tourists were avenged with a 10–0 trouncing of the same team a few days later. Scotland returned across the Atlantic having won 17 of their 18 games, scoring 99 goals and conceding just 17 in the process.

— SGIAN DUBH QUOTE —

Hagi is a brilliant player, but we're not going to get psychedelic over him.

Andy Roxburgh (former Scotland manager)

Scottish International born this day – 26 August
Donald Sandison (Don) Masson (1946)

— BARRY RAMMY – EUROPEAN CHAMPIONSHIP QUALIFYING — PLAY-OFF 2ND LEG, WEDNESDAY, 17 NOVEMBER 1999

This was Craig Brown's sixth anniversary as the nation's manager (his 57th match in that position). Scotland came to Wembley 2–0 down from the first leg played at Hampden Park the previous Saturday.

Brown had called Rangers winger Neil McCann into the side to play alongside Billy Dodds in an effort to find the finishing power that was conspicuous by its absence in the first leg.

England did not manage a single shot on target in the entire 90 minutes and coach Kevin Keegan admitted it was a dismal display. 'We would be the first to admit we did not play well. We could not get going. There are lots of excuses to make, maybe it was a bit too much for the players psychologically, having a 2–0 lead.'

Scotland looked worthy of taking the game to extra-time as they

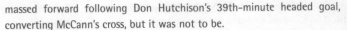

massed forward following Don Hutchison's 39th-minute headed goal, converting McCann's cross, but it was not to be.

Brown said, 'We deserved more than one goal and we played better than England did on Saturday [the first leg] ... I've never lost two in a row and I wasn't going to against England.'

The match was certainly an epic. In front of 75,848 people, seemingly mostly from north of the border, the Scots launched a ferocious riposte, looking to claw back the first-leg deficit.

Michael Owen had seemed to put the play-off beyond the Scots' reach a few minutes before Hutchison's opener, but his effort did not count, as goalkeeper Neil Sullivan had been fouled.

However, Scotland dominated England, overrunning the home side in every aspect of the game and across the field of play. England seemed devastated by the fierceness of the dark-blue onslaught and after the goal panic blighted the English ranks.

Scotland thoroughly deserved to be in front as England seemed culpable of the one offence that manager Kevin Keegan pledged his side would not succumb to – complacency.

In the first half Keegan's men produced little of any merit, although Paul Scholes shaved the side netting following Colin Hendry missing a low cross from Alan Shearer.

However, except for the form of Sol Campbell, who looked threatening on the break and secure in defence, England were overawed and over-run for most of the duration of the match.

The Scottish passion was exemplified by the bloodied face of midfielder Craig Burley, who momentarily left his side with 10 men when he had to go off the field for treatment after 56 minutes, having received a blow on the nose.

In Burley's absence, England produced their best move of the match; Owen darted on to Paul Ince's slip pass into the Scottish box, but the diminutive striker was foiled by John Collins, with a remarkable all-or-nothing tackle, executed with a fine mixture of skill and focused aggression.

But overall Owen did not impress and Keegan brought on Emile Heskey to replace him after 65 minutes, looking to provide his side with more strike power.

With just 10 minutes of the game left, Brown went for broke, sending the 19-year-old Celtic striker Mark Burchill into the fray for McCann.

A Hutchison free-kick worried the English defence minutes before a right-foot curler from Beckham went just wide of the left-hand post.

With 10 minutes left on the clock, Seaman then came to the rescue of his country, making an incredible point-blank save from Christian Dailly's header.

The Tartan Army smashed out a moving rendition of 'Flower of Scotland' as hope faded and once more they were left with just the moral victory. Keegan knew he was lucky to have come away with qualification, saying of his side, 'It was a poor performance and you have to give credit to Scotland and Craig Brown. They took a chance, they had to, and we could not get the ball off them.'

SCOTLAND	CAPS	CLUB	GOALS	ENGLAND
Neil Sullivan	13	Wimbledon		David Seaman
David Weir	19	Everton		Sol Campbell
Callum Davidson	11	Blackburn Rovers		Philip Neville
Christian Dailly	20	Blackburn Rovers		Paul Ince
Colin Hendry (Captain)	44	Rangers		Tony Adams
Barry Ferguson	5	Rangers		Gareth Southgate
Billy Dodds	15	Dundee United		David Beckham
Craig Burley	36	Celtic		Paul Scholes (Ray Parlour, 90)
Neil McCann (Burchill, 74)	5	Rangers		Alan Shearer (Captain)
Don Hutchison	7	Everton	39	Michael Owen (Emile Heskey, 63)
John Collins	58	Everton		Jamie Redknapp
Mark Burchill (McCann, 74)	4	Celtic		Ray Parlour (Paul Scholes, 90)

Referee: Pierluigi Collina (Italy)

Scottish Internationals born this day – 27 August
William Alexander Dickson (1866); James Nisbet (1904);
Edward Devlin (Eddie) Connachan (1935);
Stephen (Steve) Wright (1971)

— SGIAN DUBH QUOTE —

The underdogs will start favourites for this match.

Craig Brown (former Scotland manager)

Scottish Internationals born this day – 28 August
Stewart Mackie Houston (1949); Duncan Nichol Shearer (1962);
Kevin McNaughton (1982)

— SALTIRE SEMINAR —

Only a last-minute penalty-kick by Jimmy Delaney against Belgium at Hampden on 23 January 1946 preserved Scotland's unbeaten home record against foreign opposition. Although Switzerland took a first-half lead at Hampden on 15 May, they too failed to win, all Scotland's goals in their 3–1 success coming before half-time.

Scottish Internationals born this day – 29 August
Thomas McInnes (1870); Stephen (Steve) Clarke (1963)

— SGIAN DUBH QUOTE —

I was in Moldova airport and I went into the duty-free shop – and there wasn't a duty-free shop.

Andy Gray (20 caps)

— BALLY RAMMY – WEMBLEY WIZARDS OF '67 —

On 15 April 1967, the Home International game between Scotland and England was also part of the European Championship group 8 schedule. As such, this usually emotive game between two of the greatest rivals in international football took on even more significance.

Scotland came to London to meet the strongest opposition in their European Championship qualifying group. They were to come away with a fine victory against what was the most powerful team on the planet in front of a crowd of 99,063.

The 3–2 defeat of the then World Champions was not enough for Scotland to win their group, and it would be seven years before Scotland again qualified for a major tournament, even though the Scottish team and the players available for selection were probably never better (and would never be again).

Scotland's triumph at Wembley was the first taste of defeat England had experienced since their historic victory in 1966. Bob Brown's men who ran on to the Wembley pitch on 15 April 1967 included four players who would go on to win European Cup winners medals in Lisbon a month later, and two of the Rangers side that would be defeated by Bayern Munich in the European Cup Winners Cup Final that same week. Three other players, Jim Baxter, Denis Law and Billy Bremner, would be in anyone's all-time greatest Scotland XI. But, despite the quality of the Scottish side, they were the underdogs that day at Wembley, as the English team were the same side that had beaten West Germany just nine months earlier (apart from Jimmy Greaves being preferred over Roger Hunt) and were looking to extend a series of 19 matches without defeat.

Prior to the match, Bobby Brown, who was new to the post of national manager (it was his first game in charge), caused consternation by selecting goalkeeper Ronnie Simpson. The Celtic player was 36 years old and the game at Wembley would be his international debut. Many thought that Kilmarnock's Bobby Ferguson (who would later join West Ham United for a goalkeeper record fee) was the obvious choice. The *Glasgow Herald* reminded its readers that Frank Haffey was the last Celtic keeper to play at Wembley six years earlier and that he let in nine goals.

For all this, the nimble veteran gave a fine first performance for his country and was in no way culpable for the goals scored by Jack Charlton and Geoff Hurst.

Injuries to the future 'Lisbon Lions' Bobby Murdoch and Jimmy Johnstone were two harsh blows. Johnstone had scored twice against the English the last time the teams had met at Hampden, when England won 4–3.

Ron McKinnon of Rangers kept Billy McNeill out of the side after the Celtic captain missed previous matches through injury. Sheffield Wednesday's Jim McCalliog made his international debut, and would mark the occasion scoring his country's third goal.

Prior to the game, the Scots were fired up for the coming encounter. The Anglos were especially enthusiastic after being taunted in dressing rooms since

England had won the Jules Rimet Trophy. Famously Denis Law was unable to watch the World Cup Final even on TV and went out to play golf, muttering, 'Bastards' on hearing that the 'Auld Enemy' were the new world champions.

During the match, Law's lust for vengeance was obvious, as the Manchester United forward seemed to be at the centre of everything and forced Scotland's opener after 27 minutes, having picked up a rebound from a Willie Wallace drive.

However, another Anglo, Jim Baxter, who had joined Sunderland from Rangers in 1965, so one story has it, was studying form in the *Racing Post* a few minutes before the match. Mythology tells how, when the Scotland trainer asked him if he'd like to warm up, 'Slim Jim' stretched out his left leg and then his right and exclaimed, attention still fixed to the *Post*, 'That's me warmed up.' There could be some truth in this tale, as midfield maestro Jim did rather stroll through what was a frenzied game.

Scotland's win was founded on individual genius but also a solid and disciplined defence. Full-backs Tommy Gemmell and Eddie McCreadie were able to support Wallace and Lennox on the wings as England manager Alf Ramsey stuck by the style of play that gave rise to his World Cup-winning team's nickname, the 'Wingless Wonders', hoisting long balls forward looking for Hurst and Greaves. However, the English forwards had little joy, confronted as they were by the daunting duo of Greig and McKinnon.

An injury to Jack Charlton after his tackle on Lennox early in the first half certainly didn't help England's cause. Although the Leeds United centre-half remained on the pitch for the whole of the match, playing for the most part a forward role, he was unable to break into a committed run, but he did score England's opener.

What was to become known as the second 'Wembley Wizards' match was certainly a game of its time and place. Both sides made long runs forward with the ball, usually unchallenged and shot at goal from great distances, while team-mates were in far more likely scoring positions. The shapes of the teams were flexible, for example, Denis Law and Bobby Charlton fell back to pick up the ball from outside their own penalty areas on several occasions. The majority of the tackles if replicated today would certainly result in yellow or instant red cards.

The following Monday, Glyn Edwards, in the *Herald* (the newspaper that would become the *Sun*), wrote, 'I shall cherish for a long time the memory

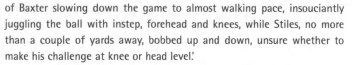

of Baxter slowing down the game to almost walking pace, insouciantly juggling the ball with instep, forehead and knees, while Stiles, no more than a couple of yards away, bobbed up and down, unsure whether to make his challenge at knee or head level.'

However, the juggling, which in the memory was a performance in itself, in reality, only lasted a couple of seconds and was not as remarkable as the fact that somebody was slowing the pace and looking for the best pass in a game wherein emotion and passion had taken over.

The result made Scotland the winners of the Home International tournament of 1967, but they missed a quarter-final match against Spain in the European Championships of 1968 due to poor results in other matches. The Scots lost in Belfast to Northern Ireland and could only draw with England at Hampden the following February. Scotland finished the group on eight points, one behind the winners, England.

England manager: Alfred Ramsey
Scotland manager: Robert Brown

SCOTLAND	CAPS	CLUB	GOALS	ENGLAND	GOALS
Ronnie Simpson	1	Celtic		Gordon Banks	
Tommy Gemmell	4	Celtic		George Reginald Cohen	
Eddie McCreadie	10	Chelsea		Ramon Wilson	
John Greig (Captain)	21	Rangers		Norbert Peter Stiles	
Ronnie McKinnon	9	Rangers		Robert Frederick Chelsea Moore (Captain)	
Jim Baxter	32	Sunderland		John (Jack) Charlton	84
William Wallace	4	Celtic		Alan James Ball	
Billy Bremner	10	Leeds United		James Peter Greaves	
Jim McCalliog	1	Sheffield Wednesday	87	Robert Charlton	
Denis Law	37	Manchester United	27	Geoffrey Charles Hurst	88
Bobby Lennox	2	Celtic	78	Martin Stanford Peter	

Referee: Gerhard Schulenburg (West Germany)

Scottish International born this day – 30 August
Peter Grant (1965)

Scottish Internationals born this day – 31 August
Stewart James Kennedy (1949); Derek Whyte (1968)

— SGIAN DUBH QUOTE —

One moment I'm playing football and the next – whack – I wake up in hospital unconscious.

Alan Brazil (13 caps)

Scottish Internationals born this day – 1 September
Robert (Bobby) Flavell (1921); William (Billy) Richie (1936)

— SALTIRE SEMINAR —

Despite the favourable April weather when the Americans visited Glasgow in 1952, their centre-half Charlie Colombo wore a pair of leather gloves throughout the game.

Scottish International born this day – 2 September
Adam Smith Blacklaw (1937)

Scottish Internationals born this day – 3 September
James Douglas (1859); James (Jimmy) Delaney (1914);
William John (Willie) Bell (1937)

Scottish International born this day – 4 September
John Archie (Johnny) McKenzie (1925)

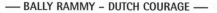

— BALLY RAMMY – DUTCH COURAGE —

A crowd of 50,670 came to Hampden Park on 15 November 2003 with cautious expectation about their side's chances in the European Championship qualifying play-off, first-leg match against the mighty Dutch. And the home side were given a scare before the first minute of the game was played out. From a low free-kick by Andy van der Meyde, Patrick Kluivert flipped a threatening-looking ball just wide of the Scottish goal.

During the swift exchanges at the start of the game, Edwin van der Sar, the visitors' keeper, managed to foil long-range efforts from McFadden and Barry Ferguson with no trouble.

At the other end, Gary Naysmith was obliged to make a crucial tackle when van der Meyde found space on the edge of the Scottish penalty area.

An intelligent move that implicated Darren Fletcher, Ferguson and Dickov split the Dutch defence and the resulting lightning cross produced a corner which led to the only goal of the game after 20 minutes.

When McFadden's original delivery came back to him, he contrived a neat one-two with Fletcher and let loose a thunderbolt of a shot that missiled into the Dutch rigging via a mean deflection.

Holland responded quickly and a close-range Jaap Stam header brought the best from Rab Douglas and he did well to save another shot from van der Meyde that sailed over the crossbar.

Lee Wilkie was Scotland's saviour with a well-timed tackle to end another thrust into the penalty area from van der Meyde. Wilkie then made a goal-line clearance after Douglas had mishandled a cross.

Christian Dailly, who would miss the return leg after picking up a yellow card, blocked a drive by Kluivert and Naysmith and followed this up by stopping a Frank de Boer header on the goal-line as the Dutch drove forward with a threatening determination in the second half.

Indeed, just two minutes after the interval, Douglas had to make a good save from a Ruud van Nistelrooy header, following more focused skill from van der Meyde.

Scotland were pinned back for long periods and were finding it difficult to deter the Dutch in midfield.

A strongly hit shot from Stam rocketed over the crossbar and Naysmith made yet another fine block to deny a clear sight of the goal to van der Meyde.

With 27 minutes of the match remaining, van der Meyde's shot struck the bar and bounced into the appreciative arms of Douglas and, shortly after, substitute Rafael van der Vaart saw the Celtic goalie gather his strike with poise.

Clarence Seedorf, another Dutch sub, let loose a dangerous-looking shot from the edge of the box. It went close, but the Scots survived.

The match was 78 minutes old when substitutes Kenny Miller and Stephen Pearson colluded to get in behind the Dutch defence, but the young Motherwell player's volley under pressure went narrowly wide.

Ferguson made Van der Sar show his class with a 20-yard drive before Jackie McNamara and Wilkie combined to stifle Van Nistelrooy in front of goal. Wilkie cleared the danger when Douglas dropped a shot from van der Meyde in the last four minutes.

The game was Berti Vogts's 20th as Scotland manager and James McFadden's first-half goal had given Scotland a chance of reaching the 2004 European Championship Finals in Greece. But, as history shows, it was not to be. However, the Everton youngster had upset the odds and the Scots had defended with great resolve. The visitors hit the woodwork and Scotland made two goal-line clearances as they worked valiantly to protect their lead. The Dutch spent most of the second half camped in and around the Scottish penalty area but the home side held firm for a famous win, riding their luck against the nation ranked fifth best in the world.

Booked – Scotland: McFadden, Dailly.
Booked – Holland: Ooijer, Stam.

Scotland coach: Hans-Hubert (Berti) Vogts
Holland coach: Dick Advocaat

SCOTLAND	CAPS	CLUB	GOALS	HOLLAND
Robert Douglas	14	Celtic		Edwin van der Sar
Jackie McNamara	22	Celtic		André Ooijer
Gary Naysmith	20	Everton		Jaap Stam
Steven Pressley	14	Heart of Midlothian		Frank de Boer (Captain)
Lee Wilkie	9	Dundee		Giovanni van Bronckhorst (Clarence Seedorf, 46)
Barry Ferguson (Captain)	20	Blackburn Rovers		Phillip Cocu
Darren Fletcher	3	Manchester United		Andy van der Meyde
Christian Dailly	49	West Ham United		Edgar Davids (Rafael van der Vaart, 60)
Paul Dickov (Miller, 65)	6	Leicester City		Ruud van Nistelrooy
James McFadden (Hutchison, 89)	8	Everton	22	Patrick Kluivert (Roy Makaay, 76)
Neil McCann (Pearson, 70)	19	Southampton		Marc Overmars
Stephen Pearson (McCann, 70)	1	Motherwell		Roy Makaay (Patrick Kluivert, 76)
Kenny Miller (Dickov, 65)	7	Wolverhampton Wanderers		Rafael van der Vaart (Edgar Davids, 60)
Don Hutchison (McFadden, 89)	26	West Ham United		Clarence Seedorf (Giovanni van Bronckhorst, 46)

Referee: Terje Hauge (Norway)

Scottish International born this day – 5 September
Henry Allan (1877)

— A WEE JOKE —

Q. How do you make an England fan run?
A. Build a job centre.

Scottish Internationals born this day – 6 September
Alexander Archibald (1897);
Kenneth Campbell (1892); Bruce David Rioch (1947);
Patrick Kevin Francis Michael (Pat) Nevin (1963);
Brian O'Neil (1972)

— SIR ALEX —

Although Alex Ferguson was an able manager of Scotland, he never gained a full cap for his country. However, he is likely to be remembered internationally as one of the great managers of the modern era.

> *He's a gent from Monday to Friday ... then on Saturday, out comes the beast.*
>
> **Paul Ince describing Sir Alex's management style**

Sir Alex's Wisdom

It's a conflict of parallels.

The lads ran their socks into the ground.

Nowhere in Europe, especially the world ...

Cole should be scoring from those distances, but I'm not going to single him out.

If we can play like that every week. we'll get some level of consistency.

This pilot move by FIFA will take root and fly.

The philosophy of a lot of European teams, even in home matches, is not to give a goal away.

It was particularly pleasing that our goalscorers scored tonight.

Scottish Internationals born this day – 7 September
George Robertson (1915);
Robert (Bobby) Johnstone (1929); Desmond George Bremner (1952);
Raymond Strean McDonald (Ray) Stewart (1959)

— SGIAN DUBH QUOTE —

There are places to this day where prejudice between Saxon and Celt dies hard, even if we can occasionally laugh about it. I like the one about the man taken ill on the train going up to Scotland. He gets out at Glasgow and asks a passer-by the quickest way to the hospital. 'See that bar yonder,' says the fellow, 'go in there and sing Danny Boy!'

John Cornwell, *The Times*

Scottish International born this day – 8 September
David Stewart (1874)

— BERSERKER BIOG – KENNY MILLER —

A centre-forward, born in Edinburgh on 23 December 1979, in a relatively short career, Kenny has played for Hibernian, Stenhousemuir on loan, Rangers and Wolves. In July 2006, he became just the third player since the War to have played for both sides of the Old Firm – following Alfie Conn and Maurice Johnston.

Miller started his career at Hutchinson Vale BC, a local league team in Edinburgh; Derek Riordan, Gary Naysmith, Steven Caldwell and Gary Caldwell also played for Vale. Miller signed for Hibernian and made his debut for the club in 1997. He was their top scorer in 1999/2000, when he joined Rangers for a fee of £2m.

In 2001, Kenny was transferred from Rangers to Wolves. The moved started as a loan deal, but was made permanent with a £3m fee. On 25 April 2001, Miller played his first full international in the WKS Zawisza Stadium, Bydgoszcz, and produced a good performance in the 1–1 draw with Poland.

In 2002/03, Kenny scored for Scotland against Germany and Iceland. In 2004, he netted his first Premiership goal, the only goal of the game against Manchester United. Despite this performance, Wolves were relegated from the Premiership after only one campaign in the top flight.

The 2004/05 season brought more international goals for Miller, against Austria, Italy and a couple against Norway.

Kenny played over 190 games for Wolves and had scored more than 60 goals during his five years with the club, when, at the end of the 2005/06 season, his contract expired and he joined Celtic under the Bosman ruling. He took some time to score his first goal for the Bhoys but ironically it came in an Old Firm match at Celtic Park in September 2006. Miller also hit the back of the net (with a penalty) in Celtic's 1–0 Champions League victory over FC Copenhagen; he scored two more European goals in the 3–0 win over Benfica.

Miller has a total of 32 caps and has scored nine times for his country.

Scottish International born this day – 9 September
Thomas Waddell (1870)

— A WEE JOKE —

Q. What's the difference between an England fan and a supermarket trolley?
A. The trolley has a mind of its own.

Scottish International born this day – 10 September
Stephen McManus (1982)

— SGIAN DUBH QUOTE —

The Jacobite rebellion was crushed by the English, but what we can't win in war we will win in football. It's payback time.
Scottish fan before an England v Scotland game

Scottish Internationals born this day – 11 September
John Greig (1942); John Spencer (1970)

—— BARRY RAMMY – BRILLIANT ORANGE ——

Scotland have played the Netherlands on 16 occasions. Half a dozen of those games have been Scottish victories, with six defeats.

On 11 June 1978, in front of a crowd of 35,130 at Estadio San Martin, Mendoza, Scotland needed to win by three clear goals to qualify from the first round of the World Cup Finals in Argentina. This was a big ask against a Dutch team famed for its 'Total Football'. Before the game the Dutch keeper Jongbloed gave Scotland every chance of achieving this feat, 'but not in 90 minutes'.

Early in the game, after Neeskens was carried off on a stretcher, Rensenbrink converted a penalty for Holland.

Playing in his first game of the tournament, Graeme Souness made a significant difference to the Scottish team. It was his lob that was headed down for Dalglish to spin and score the equaliser just before half-time.

Following the break, Souness was flattened in the penalty area, and Archie Gemmill erased memories of Masson's missed penalty against Peru earlier in the competition; Archie scored with what felt and looked like the perfect spot-kick. An exciting contest was then on. Dalglish and Jordan both headed inches wide before Gemmill, in the 68th minute, swooped on the ball after Dalglish had lost possession and weaved his way into the Dutch penalty area. Gliding round three defenders, Archie switched the ball from his right to his left foot, and shot. Many commentators saw his goal as the best of the tournament. It put Scotland 3–1 up and with over 20 minutes of play left there was still hope.

However, three minutes later, the mercurial Johnny Rep netted from 25 yards and the Scots were left with what looked like an impossible task. But the beating of Holland 3–2 was an emotive performance and Scotland's football reputation was restored, at least in part, after what had been a disappointing competition.

Scotland manager: Alistair MacLeod
Holland coach: Ernst Happel

SCOTLAND	CAPS	CLUB	GOALS	HOLLAND	GOALS
Alan Rough	21	Partick Thistle		Jan Jongbloed	
Willie Donachie	32	Manchester City		Willem Lourens Johannes Suurbier	
Martin Buchan Bruce	31	Manchester United		Rudolf Jozef Krol	
Rioch (Captain)	24	Derby County		Wilhelmus Gerardus Rijsbergen (Pieter Wildschut, 46)	
Kenny Dalglish	57	Liverpool	43	Jan Poortvliet	
Joe Jordan	33	Manchester United		Wilhelmus Antonius van de Kerkhof	
Asa Hartford	27	Manchester City		Johannes Jacobus Neeskens (Johannes Boskamp, 10)	
Stuart Kennedy	5	Aberdeen		Wilhelmus Marinus Anthonius Jansen	
Tom Forsyth	22	Rangers		Reinier Lambertus van de Kerkhof	
Archie Gemmill	29	Nottingham Forest	47 P; 68	Nicolaas Rep,	71
Graeme Souness	7	Liverpool		Pieter Robert Resenbrink	34 P

Referee: Erich Linemayr (Austria)

Scottish International born this day – 12 September
Stephan (Steve) Caldwell (1980)

— A WEE JOKE —

Q. What do you call an England fan with an IQ of 10?
A. Supremely gifted!

— SALTIRE SEMINAR —

On 27 May 1929 in Oslo, Scotland defeated a Norwegian XI 4–0 in an unofficial match in front of a crowd of 12,000 with goals from Bob Rankin (2), Jimmy Fleming and Jim Nisbet.

Scottish Internationals born this day – 13 September
Thomas Somerville Tait (1879); Patrick Gordon (Pat) Stanton (1944)

Scottish International born this day – 14 September
Alexander James (1901)

— SGIAN DUBH QUOTE —

*If I have a single image of what it means to be Scottish, I would
base it on the tartan-clad fans I met in Brussels four years ago.
We had gathered for our ritual, plucky-but-futile attempt to reach
the World Cup Finals. The Belgian Police, fearing a repeat of the
Heysel Stadium horrors of 1985, were out in strength, grim and
determined. The Scots were out for fun, however, and spotted a
particularly attractive young female officer, formed a circle round
her (and her baffled colleagues) and serenaded the young lass to
a selection of hits from* The Sound of Music. *Thus, dressed in
knee-length kilts, climbing boots and Loch Ness monster hats, the
flowers of Scotland wooed the bemused flower of Belgium's police
while singing 'Doe, a deer, a female deer ...' Sights like that can do
permanent mental damage.*

Robin McKie, the *Guardian*

Scottish International born this day – 15 September
Archibald Clark (Archie) Robertson (1929)

— BERSERKER BIOG – DARREN BARR FLETCHER —

Sir Alex Ferguson has often referred to Darren (known as 'Fletch' both to
playing colleagues and supporters) as the 'future' of Manchester United,
calling him a 'talisman'. Born 1 February 1984 in Dalkeith, Midlothian,
Fletcher joined Manchester United as a trainee in July 2000 and signed as
a professional in February 2001. Initially seen as a right-winger in the
David Beckham style, he was a highly rated prospect. Evolving into a

central midfielder, Barry started to claim a place in the Manchester United first team in the 2003/04 season, playing a number of crucial games, including a start in United's FA Cup Final win over Millwall in May 2004.

On 1 January 2005, Fletcher got his first goal at club level (he had scored twice for Scotland), the first in the Premiership match against Middlesbrough.

Darren has established himself as a regular for Scotland. He made his debut in the Ullevaal Stadium, Oslo, in the 0–0 draw with Norway on 20 August 2003, but scored a sensational goal against Lithuania, having come off the bench for only his second cap. This took Scotland to the play-offs for Euro 2004. On 26 May 2004, Darren captained Scotland to a 1–0 friendly win against Estonia in the A. Le Coq Arena, Tallinn. This made him the youngest Scotland captain since John Lambie (aged just 17 years and 92 days) of Queen's Park skippered the team that defeated Ireland 7–2 on Saturday, 20 March 1886.

Fletcher's improvement for the Scottish side was emphasised by a titanic 30-yard drive on 12 October 2005 in the World Cup qualifier in the Arena Petrol, Celje, against Slovenia. With a subtle flick and accurate half-volley, he smashed the ball into the top corner of the net to give Scotland a 1–0 advantage in a game they would eventually win 3–0. He has played 30 times for Scotland and scored four goals.

Scottish International born this day – 16 September
Daniel Doyle (1864)

— A WEE JOKE —

Four surgeons are taking a tea break and having a chat. The first surgeon says, 'Accountants are the best to operate on because, when you open them up, everything inside is numbered.'

The second surgeon says, 'Nope, librarians are the best. Everything inside them is in alphabetical order.'

The third surgeon says, 'Well, you should try electricians. Everything inside them is colour coded.'

The fourth surgeon says, 'I prefer England fans. They're heartless, spineless, gutless and their heads and arses are interchangeable.'

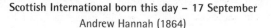

Scottish International born this day – 17 September
Andrew Hannah (1864)

— SGIAN DUBH QUOTE —

Not all breeds of genetically engineered athletes were accepted. For the 2224 World Cup, Scotland fielded a goalkeeper who was a human oblong of flesh, 24 foot by 8 that filled the entire goal. Somehow they still failed to qualify for the second round.

Grant Naylor, *Red Dwarf: Better Than Life*

Scottish International born this day – 18 September
Thomas (Tommy) Ewing (1937)

— BARRY RAMMY – HONOURS EVEN —

A crowd of 71,000 turned up at Hampden Park for the meeting between England and Scotland on 14 April 1923. John Crockett of the *Daily Mail* was enthusiastic about a prolific Scots striker: 'Andrew Wilson is always a great centre-forward before his own folk. He was in this game. He seldom wasted a ball and after he scored his shooting was terrific. When it came to a question of a personal tackle Wilson was not afraid to use his broad shoulders. He was full of cute moves and the way he got the ball so often out to Morton – well, it was the real art of centre-forward play, of which Wilson remains the greatest exponent of modern-day football.'

For all this, the report shows that Scottish supporters might have been wondering what had happened to Wilson before he netted his side's equaliser in the second half: 'He had achieved less in the first half, for his namesake on the English side had never left him.'

Indeed, George Wilson had been a virtual shadow to the Middlesbrough man.

From the start, England looked weak on the defensive left flank, where Sam Wadsworth from Huddersfield Town and West Ham's Jack Tresadern were failing to replicate their club form and were overawed by the Scottish right-wing pair. Crockett was uncompromising in his analysis: 'This, of course, was a very big football occasion and I feel it was rather too important for these two men.'

The Liverpool inside-left Harry Chambers looked England's most intelligent forward and he struck up a highly successful partnership with newcomer Fred Tunstall, on the wing. For Crockett, 'Chambers showed the brain of the football master in all he did ... He "made" England's two goals and was as good as any forward on the field.'

But he eulogised about the Scottish forward-line: 'Every man in it was clever, and those of us from the south were greatly taken with Lawson. His speed and daring led up to many a raid. The same, with foot trickery added, can be said of the incomparable Morton.'

There were no goals for half an hour, but, as the last third of the first-half emerged over the horizon of time, George Wilson, the English skipper, intercepted a pass destined for the man he was marking, and found Henry Chambers with a forward pass. The Liverpool craftsman left a trio of defenders floundering before sliding the ball out to Ted Tunstall, and the bold Blades man sent a well-weighted cross to the head of Bob Kelly who put the visitors in front.

However, a sloppy back-pass by Tresadern was picked up by Denis Lawson in a flash, and he crossed from the by-line. Ted Taylor, the English keeper, handled the ball but fumbled and wartime Hammer Andy Cunningham was quick to punish and make the score 1–1.

Before half-time, England were in front again. Chambers found Tunstall out on the wing, and the Sheffield lad belted down the flank before crossing, for West Ham's Vic Watson to score.

Shortly after the interval, Andy Wilson fell on a loose ball gyrating towards left-back Wadsworth, who made the lethal error of wavering. Wilson grabbed his opportunity and ran on to score.

Although England had taken the lead twice by the final whistle, the southerners knew they had been lucky to share the honours with a superior Scottish side.

As Tresadern often said in later years, 'I was the best player Scotland had on the field.' But he served his country better as part of the side that defeated Sweden in Stockholm the following month when his fellow Hammer Billy Moore scored two of the goals in a 1–3 victory. However, it was to be the last cap Tres would be awarded.

SCOTLAND	CAPS	CLUB	GOALS	ENGLAND	GOALS	CLUB
William Harper	3	Hibernian		Edward Hallows Taylor		Huddersfield Town
John Hutton	3	Aberdeen		Ephraim Longworth		Liverpool
James Blair	7	Cardiff City		Samuel John Wadsworth		Huddersfield Town
David Steele	3	Huddersfield Town		Frederick William Kean		Sheffield Wednesday
William Cringan (Captain)	5	Celtic		George Wilson (Captain)		Sheffield Wednesday
Thomas Muirhead	2	Rangers		John Tresadern		West Ham United
Denis Lawson	1	St Mirren		Samuel B. Chedgzoy		Everton
Andrew Cunningham	6	Rangers	35	Robert F. Kelly	31	Burnley
Andrew Wilson	12	Middlesbrough	55	Victor Martin Watson	42	West Ham United
Thomas Cairns	4	Rangers		Henry Chambers		Liverpool
Alan Morton	8	Rangers		Frederick Edward Tunstall		Sheffield United

Referee: Arthur Ward (England)

Scottish International born this day – 19 September
John Divers (1873)

Scottish International born this day – 20 September
Hugh Morgan (1869)

Scottish Internationals born this day – 21 September
William Sturrock Maxwell (1876); John McDougall (1901)

Scottish Internationals born this day – 22 September
James (Jim) Forest (1944); Thomas (Tommy) Hutchison (1947);
James (Jimmy) Bone (1949)

— BERSERKER BIOG - LEE HENRY MCCULLOCH —

Born 14 May 1978 in Bellshill, McCulloch was a teenage forward with Motherwell in the Scottish Premier League in 1996. A healthy strike rate caused Wigan Athletic to pay £700,000 to take him to the JJB Stadium in March 2001, at that point a club record for the Latics, when they were playing their football in the third tier of the English game. But competing at a lower level gave Lee the opportunity to develop his skills. He is now more a midfielder than an out-and-out striker, but in the club's first season in the top flight (2005/06) he grabbed five League goals in 30 appearances, helping Wigan to a 10th place at the conclusion of their historic initial campaign in the Premiership.

In January 2007, Rangers made £750,000 bid for Lee. But the then Wigan manager Paul Jewell called the offer 'derisory'.

McCulloch told BBC Sport in May 2007 that he wanted to play for Rangers and on 23 June Rangers offered £1.5m for his services, but Wigan wanted something like £1m more to part with McCulloch.

On 11 July 2007, it was revealed that Rangers had agreed on an undisclosed fee (believed to be around £2.25m) with Wigan that would take McCulloch to Ibrox Park.

Lee made his international debut in the Republican Stadium, Chisinau, on 13 October in 2004 during a FIFA World Cup qualifier, coming on as a late substitute in a 1–1 draw with Moldova. He now has 11 caps.

— SALTIRE SEMINAR —

In the 1929 Scotland v England match at Hampden Park, Alex Cheyne's goal was scored directly from a corner kick two years after the law was changed to allow goals direct from corners, but was the first to be credited in an international match. However, this was not the only unusual incident of the game. An indirect free-kick was awarded under the new law that dictated that the goalkeeper was not allowed to carry the ball more than four steps. Confusion took over and the Scottish players lined up behind the ball, rather than on their own goal-line. However, they did manage to sort out defensive cover and cleared their lines.

Scottish Internationals born this day – 23 September
Andrew Black (1917); David Wedderburn (Dave) Gibson (1938);
James (Jim) McCalliog (1946); Kenneth (Kenny) Burns (1953)

— BARRY RAMMY – INTERNATIONAL VICTORY —

To celebrate the end of World War I, two 'Victory' matches between England and Scotland were arranged, to be played within the eight days of each other. The first encounter between the two nations was played at Goodison Park, Liverpool, on 26 April 1919 (these matches were not to be considered part of the official record). It was an unusually clean game (only four fouls were recorded during the match, all for minor infringements) and as a consequence was seen by some as lacking the aggression so often the product of the passion that was a feature of this premier British football conflict. Alfred Davis in the *Daily Mail* commented, 'Both teams had reason to be satisfied with a capital match, although one or two reputations suffered.'

But perhaps four years of war had mellowed some of those involved and/or put things into perspective.

Davis saw the game going the visitors' way in the first part of the match: 'For 20 minutes Scotland appeared to have the game well in hand. They played with fine confidence and skill in establishing a lead of two goals during that period. England found their feet after scoring the first goal shortly before the interval and playing with the wind in the second

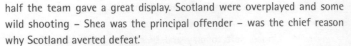

half the team gave a great display. Scotland were overplayed and some wild shooting – Shea was the principal offender – was the chief reason why Scotland averted defeat.'

The match began with Scotland playing with the wind at their backs and they went ahead within two minutes. Morton, after picking up a throw-in, sent a perfect cross to Wright who shot past the prevaricating Sam Hardy. Another Morton cross gave Jimmy Bowie an opportunity and his half-volley from 20 yards out smashed home.

This was the first time Alan Lauder Morton, then a Queen's Park amateur (the only non-professional on the park that day), had played for Scotland. The *Athletic News* told of his 'peculiar dainty feinting zigzagging style. He appears at every step to be about to dart inside, yet still holds his course.'

In the next few years, other Englishmen tried to describe and emulate that fast shuffling run; many more were to attempt to halt or even anticipate its direction; most were unsuccessful.

Morton was to be a regular in the Scottish side until he won the last of his caps in 1932. He had been a thorn in the side of any opposing team; an unrelenting ripping anxiety who bruised the confidence of a generation of English defenders. He was to tell how he learned his magic in his backyard, taking hundreds of hours to perfect lobbing, chipping or driving the ball through a small hole in a cellar door with both left and right feet. However, Morton was something better than a disciplined practitioner; he had an innate intelligence and sense for the strategy of football. Tales of his talent and guile, his swerving shots for goals, his fantastic ability to outsmart an opponent are part of mythology of Scottish football. He won 31 caps and, following his 12 years as an international (starting at Ninian Park Cardiff on 26 February 1920), many an Englishman was glad to see the back of him.

An impressive display of passing between former West Ham winger Danny Shea and Bobby Turnbull culminated with Bradford's young star scoring England's first goal just before half-time.

The second half was a tale of England struggling to find a way back into the game, while resisting the combined efforts of Morton and Celtic's Jim McMenemy, who, although he seemed to have lost a little sharpness to the War, worked well with Morton to create a threatening Scottish wing that

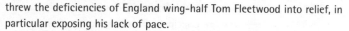

threw the deficiencies of England wing-half Tom Fleetwood into relief, in particular exposing his lack of pace.

With 15 minutes left to play and time seemingly running out for England, Syd Puddefoot found some space and, making full use of the room he was given, devised a devastating run. With the Scottish full-backs closing in on him from wide positions, the West Ham centre-forward, with immaculate timing, released the ball giving Jim Brownlie no chance with a close-range shot.

England got the draw, but the Scottish side might have counted themselves as unlucky. The best forward on the field was the winger Morton, while Scotland's right-back Alex McNair and their right-half James Eadie Gordon had been solid as England applied pressure after they had scored the equaliser.

Alf Davis summed up England's game: 'Hardy is still England's safest goalkeeper, despite the fact that he misjudged the first goal ... The backs were steady and reliable after an indifferent start and McCall and Grimsdell were fine, sturdy workers and determined tacklers at half-back. The Tottenham man was a great success in his first international.'

For all this, it had been the flash of insight and strong athleticism of Puddefoot that had saved England's blushes at the ignominy of being beaten on their own turf.

England: Hardy (Aston Villa); Longworth (Liverpool), Duckworth (Blackburn Rovers); Fleetwood (Everton), McCall (Preston North End), Grimsdell (Tottenham Hotspur); Turnbull (Bradford), Shea (Blackburn Rovers), Puddefoot (West Ham), Smith (Bolton), Martin (Sunderland).
Scotland: Brownlie (Morton); McNair (Celtic), Blair (Sheffield Wednesday); Gordon (Rangers), Wright (Morton), McMullan (Partick Thistle); Donaldson (Bolton), Bowie (Rangers), Richardson (Ayr), McMenemy (Celtic), A. Morton (Queen's Park).

Scottish Internationals born this day – 24 September
John O'Hare (1946); Robert Sime (Roy) Aitken (1958);
Murdo Davidson MacLeod (1958); Alistair Murdoch (Ally) McCoist (1962);
Thomas (Tommy) Boyd (1965); Gary John McSwegan (1970);
Craig William Burley (1971)

— SGIAN DUBH QUOTE —

He was on the six-yard line, just two yards away from the goal.

Pat Nevin (28 caps)

Scottish International born this day – 25 September
Hugh Patrick Curran (1943)

— A WEE JOKE —

Steve McLaren was wheeling his shopping trolley across the supermarket car park when he noticed an old lady struggling with her shopping.

He stopped and asked, 'Can you manage, dear?' to which the old lady replied, 'No way, you got yourself into this mess, don't ask me to sort it out!'

Scottish Internationals born this day – 26 September
George Duncan Chaplin (1888); Michael Gilhooley (1896);
Robert Brown (Bobby) Clark (1945); George Wood (1952)

— BARRY RAMMY – VICTORY II —

The second Scotland v England Victory international took place at Hampden Park. In an England-dominated first half, the Scottish defence seemed nervous and unusually tentative. At the same time, the home strikers found it hard to work as a unit, a problem that had traditionally been associated with the England side. Overall, Scotland found it difficult to get into their stride.

The Spurs wing-half Arthur Grimsdell picked up the ball from a corner and scored the first goal of the game with what one journalist called 'a hurricane shot'. He put England two in front before Puddefoot made the most of Jim McMullan's hesitancy to make the score 0–3.

In the early part of the second half, Scotland mounted a series of raids that led to the harassed English defence giving away a penalty; Andy Wilson converted. Following an impressive flank run, Morton brought his side closer to drawing level, shooting past Hardy from a tight angle. But, as tartan hopes were resuscitated, Puddefoot applied a killer blow just a few yards from the Scots' goal-line. A couple of minutes before the end of the match Wilson made the score look more respectable for the home side, but, despite continued effort, the fiery clansmen could not prevent Scotland's first home defeat since 1904, England's first victory north of the border for 15 years, the Sassenach's first-ever win on the wide open spaces of Hampden Park. But the game was a hard-fought battle, Scotland having mounted a furious onslaught in the second 45 minutes.

Scotland: J. Brownlie (Greenock Morton); McNair (Celtic), Blair (Sheffield Wednesday); Gordon (Rangers), Wright (Morton), McMullan (Partick Thistle), Reid (Airdrieonians), Bowie (Rangers), Wilson (Heart of Midlothian), McMenemy (Celtic), A. Morton (Rangers).

England: Hardy (Aston Villa); Longworth (Liverpool), Duckworth (Blackburn Rovers); Fleetwood (Everton), McCall (Preston North End), Grimsdell (Tottenham Hotspur); Turnbull (Bradford), Shea (Blackburn Rovers), Puddefoot (West Ham), J. Smith (Bolton Wanderers), Martin (Sunderland).

Scottish International born this day – 27 September
Steven Archibald (1956)

— SALTIRE SEMINAR —

Half a dozen of the Scottish team that played England in 1930 were Rangers players: Dougie Gray, Jock Buchanan, Davie Meiklejohn, 'Tully' Craig, Jimmy Fleming and Alan Morion.

Scottish International born this day – 28 September
Robert (Bobby) Hope (1943)

— BERSERKER BIOG – SCOTT DEREK SEVERIN —

Stirling-born (15 February 1979) Scott is a versatile player, having filled the role of defender and striker at club level.

He started his career at Hearts before joining Aberdeen in July 2004 when his contract expired. He has played for Scotland 15 times since making his international debut in the FIFA World Cup qualifier v Latvia on 6 October 2001 at Hampden Park (Scotland won 2–1).

> **Scottish Internationals born this day – 29 September**
> Robert Robison Kelso (1865); James Curran (Jim) Baxter (1939);
> William (Willie) Pettigrew (1953); Joseph Nicol (Nicky) Walker (1962);
> Ian Durrant (1966)

— A WEE JOKE —

Q. What's the difference between an England fan and a coconut?
A. You can get a drink out of a coconut!

> **Scottish International born this day – 30 September**
> James (Jimmy) Johnstone (1944)

— BARRY RAMMY – HALF-CENTURY OF HATE —

At Old Trafford on 17 April 1926, 49,000 expectant supporters witnessed a game that from the start exposed the difference between Scotland and England and seemed to be about both style and ability. For *The Times*: 'England certainly went near to scoring several times, but one could not ignore the fact that nearly all their attacks were spasmodic and ill-supported. From the very start there was the significant spectacle of Englishmen always running after the ball and Scotsmen nearly always on the ball or waiting for it.'

However, the performance of the England full-backs did give the home crowd something to applaud. Tom Mort did well to dominate winger Alex Jackson and the speed of his defensive partner Fred Goodall in the penalty area matched both the mercurial Hughie Gallacher and outside-left Alex Troup.

Bill Walker, the England skipper, showed his brilliance in patches, but it seemed that the effort he expended in the first-half left him wanting in the second period.

According to *The Times*, 'Most of the English efforts were charged down or lacking in steam … Scotland's shots were harder but all went over or wide.'

The only goal of the game exemplified Scotland's more meticulous attitude. Gallacher was the creator. His clever interplay with Jackson culminated with the latter collecting a perfect pass in front of goal; the England keeper Ted Taylor had no chance with the shot that rebounded into the net off the inside of a post.

In the 50th full international between the greatest of football rivals, England failed to achieve victory for the sixth year in succession. For Scotland the win meant that they had won the Home International crown. England were again at the bottom of the home table.

In its post-match analysis *The Times* searched for reasons for England's run of poor results: 'In searching for reasons for the rather humiliating position occupied by England, in spite of all her apparent wealth of first-class League clubs, one noted two outstanding facts. One of these was painfully obvious at Glasgow last year, when the slightly slower but vastly more efficient conception of the dribbling game held by Scotsmen enabled their national side not only to score two goals to none, but to outplay their opponents in the process.'

But *The Times* was not totally magnanimous: 'One might add perhaps that Scottish Association Football also had its faults; and over-elaboration and mere trickiness at times are two of them.'

For all this, *The Thunderer* was correct in pinpointing the major strength of the Scots: 'It was in the perfect positioning and backing up of their players that Scotland achieved victory.'

But another factor put forward by *The Times* for England's ignominious form was the differing attitudes of the respective sets of supporters, the zealous Scottish fans refusing to even think about defeat: 'A stranger in Manchester on Saturday night might well have fancied himself in Glasgow. Inside the ground there was the same impression of Scottish enthusiasm and comparative indifference on the part of the English spectators.'

PLAYER NAME	CAPS	CLUB	GOALS	ENGLAND	CLUB
William Harper	11	Arsenal		Edward Hallows Taylor	Huddersfield Town
John Hutton	7	Aberdeen		Frederick Roy Goodall	Huddersfield Town
William McStay (Captain)	8	Celtic		Thomas Mort	Aston Villa
James Gibson	1	Partick Thistle		Willis Edwards	Leeds United
William Summers	1	St Mirren		John Henry Hill	Burnley
James McMullan	9	Manchester City		George Henry Green	Sheffield United
Alex Jackson	6	Huddersfield Town	36	Richard Ernest York	Aston Villa
Alex Thomson	1	Celtic		Sydney Charles Puddefoot	Blackburn Rovers
Hugh Gallacher	7	Newcastle United		Edward Cashfield Harper	Blackburn Rovers
Andrew Cunningham	10	Rangers		William Henry Walker (Captain)	Aston Villa
Alex Troup	5	Everton		James William Ruffell	West Ham United

Referee: Thomas R. Dougray (Scotland)

Jimmy Gibson was the son of Neil Gibson, former Rangers and Scotland player.

Scottish Internationals born this day – 1 October
William Urquhart Baird (1874); William (Willie) McFarlane (1923);
Eric Black (1963)

— SALTIRE SEMINAR —

In October 1933 Harry McMenemy was selected for the Scottish team to play Wales. However, after he sustained an injury, his brother John was called up to replace him. It was John McMenemy's only international, while Harry would never be capped.

Scottish Internationals born this day – 2 October
Alfred (Alfie) Conn Snr. (1926); William (Willie) Morgan (1944);
John Robertson (1964); Stephen Pearson (1982)

— CALEDONIAN CHRONICLES —

In February 1988, the Scottish Football Association launched an International Roll of Honour, initially made up of the first 11 Scottish players to have been awarded 50 full caps. Each player on the Roll receives a gold medal, an invitation for life to all Scotland's home games, and has his portrait hung at the Scottish Football Museum.

There are now 25 players in the International Roll of Honour, the latest to qualify being David Weir, who passed the half-century mark in the Euro 2008 qualifier against Lithuania.

Kenny Dalglish 102
1971–1986
Celtic, Liverpool

Jim Leighton 91
1982–1998
Aberdeen (twice),
Manchester United,
Hibernian

Alex McLeish 77
1980–1993
Aberdeen

Paul McStay 76
1983–1997
Celtic

Tom Boyd 72
1990–2001
Motherwell, Chelsea, Celtic

Willie Miller 65
1975–1989
Aberdeen

Christian Dailly 65
1997 to date
Blackburn Rovers, Derby County,
West Ham United

Danny McGrain 62
1973–1982
Celtic

Richard Gough 61
1983–1993
Dundee United, Tottenham
Hotspur, Rangers

Ally McCoist 61
1985–1998
Rangers, Kilmarnock

John Collins 58
1988–1999
Hibernian, Celtic, AS Monaco,
Everton

Roy Aitken 57
1979–1991
Celtic, St. Mirren

Gary McAllister 57
1990–1999
Leicester City, Leeds United,
Coventry City

David Weir 56
1997–
Heart of Midlothian, Everton,
Rangers

Denis Law 55
1958–1974
Huddersfield Town, Manchester
City (twice), Torino, Manchester
United

Maurice Malpas 55
1984–1992
Dundee United

Billy Bremner 54
1965–1975
Leeds United

Graeme Souness 54
1974–1986
Middlesbrough, Liverpool,
Sampdoria, Rangers

George Young 53
1946–1957
Rangers

Alan Rough 53
1976–1986
Partick Thistle, Hibernian

Kevin Gallacher 53
1988–2001
Dundee United, Coventry City,
Blackburn Rovers, Newcastle United

Joe Jordan 52
1973–1982
Leeds United, Manchester United,
Milan AC

Colin Hendry 51
1993–2001
Blackburn Rovers, Rangers,
Coventry City, Bolton Wanderers

Asa Hartford 50
1972–1982
West Bromwich Albion,
Manchester City, Everton

Gordon Strachan 50
1980–1992
Aberdeen, Manchester United,
Leeds United

Scottish International born this day – 3 October
James Dougall (1913)

— SALTIRE SEMINAR —

Bob Gillespie was the last amateur to skipper Scotland when he led the team that faced England in 1933.

Scottish Internationals born this day – 4 October
Alistair Robert (Ally) Hunter (1949); James Allan (Jim) Holton (1951)

— SGIAN DUBH QUOTE —

It's what I call one of those 'indefensible ones' – you can't defend against them.

Andy Gray (20 caps)

Scottish Internationals born this day – 5 October
Thomson Sandlands Allan (1946); Andrew (Drew) Jarvie (1948);
William (Willie) Donachie (1951)

Scottish International born this day – 6 October
John Boyd (Jackie) Plendereith (1937)

— SALTIRE SEMINAR —

The Saltire

Go to any Scottish international game and you will see what is commonly known as the 'St Andrew's Cross' flag being waved around the stadium in a range of sizes. This insignia has an interesting history.

As St Andrew, one of the Apostles, was condemned to be crucified under Roman law, legend has it that he asked to be placed on a cross of a different shape from that used to execute Jesus (the Saltire). Andrew's relics (bones) were said to have been brought to Scotland following a vision to St Regulus, telling him to carry them to a far-off land. He landed at a place that was then called Muckros; later it came to be known as Kilrymont, which was renamed St Andrews.

According to myth, before a 9th- or 10th-century battle between a united Picts and Scots army and the Anglo-Saxon King of Northumbria at Athelstaneford in East Lothian, a cluster of white clouds in the form of the cross of St Andrew appeared in the sky.

The Northumbrians were beaten and St Andrew became the patron saint of Scotland. Hence, the white cross on a blue background started its history as an emblem of Scottish nationalism. In the 14th century, many Scottish foot soldiers had a white cross on their tunics but it was not until the 15th century that the national flag came into more general use.

Theoretically, only the white cross is a Saltire but that name is often applied to the complete flag.

While the explanation of its origins may be questionable, the Scottish flag is regarded as one of the oldest national flags still being used.

After King James VI of Scotland became King of England in 1603, he attempted to introduce a flag with the white cross of St Andrew and the blue background together with the red cross of St George. The Scottish Parliament furiously discarded the idea. In 1801, the red cross of St Patrick was incorporated into the Union flag and official buildings in Scotland were instructed to fly it.

— SGIAN DUBH QUOTE —

It's not true. Technically you can say it's true, yes.

Steve Archibald (27 caps)

Scottish International born this day – 7 October
John Campbell (1871)

— SALTIRE SEMINAR —

During their four-week tour of North America in 1935, under trainer Arthur Dixon, Scotland won all 12 of the games they contested. They beat Hamilton 10–1, and scored nine goals against both Calgary and Kitchener. Matches were also played against Philadelphia, New York, Toronto, Chicago, Winnipeg and Montreal.

Scottish Internationals born this day – 8 October
Henry Hogg Allan (1872); Duncan Henderson Ogilvie (1911); William
Dallas Fyfe (Bill) Brown (1931); Colin MacDonald Jackson (1946)

— BERSERKER BIOG – NIGEL FRANCIS QUASHIE —

Quashie made his League debut in December 1995 for Queens Park Rangers
against Manchester United at Old Trafford. The West Londoners were
beaten 2–1 but Nigel was impressive. He was called into the first team now
and then for the remainder of what was to be a relegation season for QPR.
Although out of the Premiership, Quashie got a regular place in the Super
Hoops' first team during the 1997/98 campaign.

It was during his initial period at Loftus Road that Quashie was called into
the England Under-21 side and he also gained 'B' international honours.

At the beginning of the 1998/99 term, Quashie joined Nottingham
Forest (then a Premiership side) for a fee of £2.5m. But he struggled to get
into the side and experienced his second relegation. Nigel did eventually
settle in at the City Ground, and showed some good form, but, after Forest
missed out on promotion, in 2000/01 Quashie moved to Portsmouth who
paid a cut-price £600,000 for his services. In 2002/03, he helped Pompey
to win the First Division Championship.

Although Nigel had played for England at Under-21 level, he was
eligible (through his Glasgow-born grandfather) to appear for Scotland
and made his full international debut at the A. Le Coq Arena, Tallinn,
against Estonia, on 27 May 2004. He scored a goal in his second game
(a 4–1 win over Trinidad and Tobago) which assured his place as a first-
team regular.

On 17 January 2005, Quashie rejoined former Portsmouth manager
Harry Redknapp at Southampton for a fee of £2.1 million. After the
transfer of Jason Dodd, he became the club's captain, but he was unable to
prevent the Saints being relegated (the third time he had gone down) at
the end of the 2004/05 season.

On 31 January 2006, Nigel moved to West Bromwich Albion for £1.2m
and at the end of the season achieved the uncommon distinction of being
relegated in two successive seasons, his fourth experience of 'the drop'.

Quashie became Alan Curbishley's second signing as West Ham manager on 8 January 2007. He came to Upton Park for a fee of £1.5m, rising to £1.7m depending on appearances.

On 13 January 2007, Nigel made his Premier League debut with the Hammers against Fulham. He has played 14 times for Scotland and scored one goal.

Scottish International born this day – 9 October
Stephen (Steve) Murray (1944)

— SGIAN DUBH QUOTE —

It's a Dutch invention, but we started it in Scotland.
Andy Roxburgh (former Scotland manager on 'Total Football')

Scottish Internationals born this day – 10 October
Paul Whitehead Sturrock (1956); Graham Alexander (1971);
Robert Scott (Scott) Dobie (1978); David McNamee (1980)

Scottish Internationals born this day – 11 October
Ronald Campbell (Ronnie) Simpson (1930); Graham Alexander (1971);
Steven Pressley (1973)

— SGIAN DUBH QUOTE —

That's bread and butter straight down the goalkeeper's throat.
Andy Gray (20 caps)

Scottish Internationals born this day – 12 October
Bernard Joseph Battles (1905); Allan Duncan Brown (1926);
Allan Evans (1956); Brian Kerr (1981)

— SALTIRE SEMINAR —

The Scottish team and its supporters share the nickname the Tartan Army.

Scottish Internationals born this day – 13 October
Peter Symington Buchanan (1915); James (Jimmy) Duncanson (1919)

Scottish Internationals born this day – 14 October
Charles (Charlie) Cooke (1942); Steven Thompson (1978)

— SGIAN DUBH QUOTE —

He'll be giving everything, but he hasn't got everything to give.

Ian St John (21 caps)

Scottish Internationals born this day – 15 October
James Kelly (1865); Robert Johnston (Bert) McCann (1932);
Warren Cummings (1980)

Scottish Internationals born this day – 16 October
James (Jimmy) Gabriel (1940); Graeme Marshall Sharp (1960)

— SALTIRE SEMINAR —

England star Raich Carter described the Hampden Roar that hit him as he was warming up before an international: 'It began with a murmur, rolling round the ground and mounting up out of nothing into a swelling, terrific roar that came at us from all sides. I wondered what had happened. Then I saw the Scotland team running out in their navy-blue shirts.'

Scottish Internationals born this day – 17 October
James Cowan (1868); Francis (Frank) Burns (1948);
David Robertson (1968)

Scottish Internationals born this day – 18 October
Thomas (Tommy) Gemmell (1943)

— SGIAN DUBH QUOTE —

They haven't lived up to the expectations we expect of them.
George Graham (12 caps)

Scottish International born this day – 19 October
Paul Hartley (1976)

Scottish Internationals born this day – 20 October
Alexander Lowson Keillor (1869); Daniel Bruce (1870);
Neil Martin (1940)

— SALTIRE SEMINAR —

When Scotland played England in April 1950, all five forwards were called
William – Waddell, Moir, Bauld, Steel, Liddell. England's goalkeeper was
Bert Williams.

Scottish International born this day – 21 October
Paul Norman Telfer (1971)

Scottish Internationals born this day – 22 October
Alan John Gilzean (1938); Craig Levein (1964);
Paul Michael Lyons McStay (1964)

— SGIAN DUBH QUOTE —

The one thing that tackle wasn't was high and dangerous.
Andy Gray (20 caps)

Scottish Internationals born this day – 23 October
David Cochrane (Dave) Mathers (1931); Colin Cameron (1972);
Christian Edward Dailly (1973)

Scottish Internationals born this day – 24 October
Richard (Asa) Hartford (1950); Jackie McNamara (1973)

Scottish Internationals born this day – 25 October
David Storrier (1872); Donald Ford (1944);
Francis Michael (Frank) Munro (1947); Russell Anderson (1978)

— BERSERKER BIOG – BARRY FERGUSON —

With 39 caps (and two goals), Glasgow-born Ferguson (2 February 1978) is one of the most experienced players in the current Scottish squad. A midfielder who skippers both Rangers and the national side, Barry has had a love for his club since he was a child, long before joining the Rangers first-team squad in 1994/95. He recently stated that he would be 'buried in the shirt'. He made his first-team debut on the last day of the 1996/97 season against Hearts and Barry was awarded the distinction of 'man of the match'. He became a permanent first-team fixture at Ibrox in the 1998/99 season.

Barry, known both to team-mates and fans as 'Bazza', became the youngest captain of Rangers in the club's history in the 2002/02 term, leading his side to a League Cup and Scottish Cup double. The following season, Ferguson skippered Rangers to a domestic treble and won the Scottish Football Writers' Association Footballer of the Year and Scottish PFA Players' Player of the Year.

At the start of the 2003/04 season Ferguson joined Blackburn Rovers for a fee of £7.5m.

Ferguson put in a transfer request after 16 months at Ewood Park, saying that the prospect of playing in the English Premiership and the odd Lancashire derby could not be compared with the thrill of taking part in an Old Firm match, and £4.5m took Barry back to Ibrox shortly before the close of the transfer window in January 2005. He was part of the Rangers team that won the League on the last day of the season.

At the age of 21 Ferguson made his international debut in a UEFA European Championship qualifier against Lithuania on 5 September 1998 in a goalless draw at the Zalgiris Stadium, Vilnius. He was also appointed captain of the national side by then manager Berti Vogts following the retirement of Paul Lambert.

Awarded the MBE on 17 June 2006, Ferguson is the only current Rangers player to be inducted into the Rangers FC Hall of Fame. Still in his peak years, Barry's list of honours from the Scottish game include:

Scottish Premier League: 1998/99, 1999/00, 2002/03, 2004/05;

Scottish Cup: 1998/99, 1999/00, 2001/02, 2002/03;

Scottish League Cup: 1998/99, 2001/02, 2002/03, 2004/05.

Scottish Internationals born this day – 26 October
William Douglas (Willie) Telfer (1925); Arthur Graham (1952)

Scottish Internationals born this day – 27 October
George Lewis Young (1922); Francis Tierney (Frank) Gray (1954);
Stuart McKimmie (1962)

— SALTIRE SEMINAR —

The Scottish Lion

At matches involving the Scottish national team, you are guaranteed to see their 'Lion' being hoisted as a standard. Similar to the emblem of the Scottish Football Association, a lion rampant, which has traditionally been worn on the Scottish international shirt, is based on the Royal standard for Scotland.

In the days when flags and banners were important to identify opposing elements in battle, King William I, The Lion (1143–1214), adopted a heraldic device showing a rampant lion, the 'king of beasts', rearing up with three paws stretched out. This became the Royal coat of arms in Scotland. The lion was also incorporated into the Great Seal of Scotland which was placed on all official documents.

When the Royal coat of arms was being designed, the lion rampant was incorporated, with the Latin motto *Nemo me impune lacessit*, meaning *No one attacks me with impunity*. In the Scottish vernacular that became *Wha daur meddle wi' me?* Pretty much on the button in terms of Scottish football.

The lion rampant flag strictly speaking belongs solely to the monarch – though a Royal warrant has been issued allowing it to be displayed as a token of loyalty to the Crown.

At one time, using the Royal coat of arms unlawfully could have meant a hefty fine ... or worse.

Scottish International born this day – 28 October
Lawrence (Lawrie) Reilly (1928)

— SGIAN DUBH QUOTE —

The Brazilians aren't as good as they used to be, or as they are now.

Kenny Dalglish (102 caps)

Scottish Internationals born this day – 29 October
Moses McLay McNeil (1855); Alexander (Alex) Wilson (1933)

Scottish Internationals born this day – 30 October
Michael Dunbar (1863); Donald Currie Sillars (1868);
Thomas Cairns (1890); Robert Primrose Wilson (1941);
Anthony (Tony) Green (1946)

— CALEDONIAN CHRONICLES – MOST CAPPED SCOTLAND PLAYERS —

	PLAYER	CLUBS	SCOTLAND CAREER	CAPS	GOALS
1	Kenny Dalglish	Celtic, Liverpool	1971–1986	102	30
2	Jim Leighton	Aberdeen, Manchester United, Hibernian	1982–1998	91	0
3	Alex McLeish	Aberdeen	1980–1993	77	0
4	Paul McStay	Celtic	1983–1997	76	9
5	Tom Boyd	Motherwell, Chelsea, Celtic	1990–2001	72	1
6	Willie Miller	Aberdeen	1975–1989	65	1
7	Christian Dailly	Blackburn Rovers, Derby County, West Ham United	1997–present	63	6
8	Danny McGrain	Celtic	1973–1982	62	0
9	Richard Gough	Dundee United, Tottenham Hotspur, Rangers	1983–1993	61	6
=	Ally McCoist	Rangers, Kilmarnock	1985–1998	61	19

'Clubs' detailed are those players were registered with when they were awarded caps.

Scottish International born this day – 31 October
Robert Neil (1876)

— SALTIRE SEMINAR —

In over 15 years of international football, Scotland scored in every match they played. The first time they failed to find the net was the 0–5 defeat by England in 1888.

Scottish Internationals born this day – 1 November
Matthew Stephen (Matt) Elliott (1968); Paul Dickov (1972)

— SGIAN DUBH QUOTE —

The one thing England have got is spirit, resolve, grit and determination.

Alan Hansen (26 caps)

Scottish International born this day – 2 November
Daniel Paton (1871)

— BERSERKER BIOG – JAMES CURRAN BAXTER —

Born on 29 September 1939 in Hill of Beath, Fife, Jim began his professional career at Raith Rovers before joining his boyhood heroes Rangers for a Scottish record transfer fee of £17,500. It was 1960 and Baxter was not yet 21. He was five years at Ibrox Park and then moved to Sunderland. In 1967, he joined Nottingham Forest, but by this time he was becoming notorious for his off-the-field activities.

Jim returned briefly to Rangers in 1969 but retired from football in 1970. He was just 30 years old and had won 34 caps for Scotland over a six-year career (he was his country's skipper on four occasions). This was a record any player would be proud of, but no one doubted that Baxter had massively underachieved given his skill and natural ability.

Jim made his Scotland debut v Northern Ireland on 9 November 1960. He is remembered in particular for his inspirational role in Scotland's triumphant 3–2 defeat of England in 1967. During a magnificent performance, Jim played 'keepie uppie', so tormenting the opposition while also showing his contempt for them. This was the Scotland side that were the first team to beat England after the 1966 World Cup, so after the game most Scots regarded their team as world champions. However, Jim thought his performance in the 1963 defeat of England at Wembley was his best against the 'Auld Enemy'. Scotland were obliged to play most of that game with 10 men; Eric Caldow's leg was broken in a tackle early on, and at that time there were no substitutes.

Baxter scored Scotland's first after winning a tackle. He netted the second by way of a penalty (Caldow had originally been the designated penalty-taker). In 2001, Jim told how up to that point he 'had never taken a penalty in my life before'.

In later life, Jim was asked whether it would have made a difference to his lifestyle if he had been paid the huge sums of money modern footballers receive. 'Definitely,' he said. 'I'd have spent £50,000 a week at the bookies instead of £100.'

Despite Baxter's behaviour beyond the field of play, his womanising, frequent drunkenness and gambling, Jim is remembered as one of the greatest Scottish players of all time, even on the evidence of just 34 caps; of course, he could and should have played many more times for Scotland.

Baxter lost a long battle against cancer on 14 April 2001.

The Tartan Army attempted to get the new Wembley footbridge named after him, which might have annoyed many of the English supporters. Scots flooded a poll held by the national Radio Five Live, but somehow he didn't make it into the final reckoning.

Scottish International born this day – 3 November
John Ritchie (1876)

— SGIAN DUBH QUOTE —

I don't think anyone enjoyed it. Apart from the people who watched it.
Alan Hansen (26 caps)

Scottish Internationals born this day – 4 November
Derek Johnstone (1953); Robert (Robbie) Winters (1974)

— CALEDONIAN CHRONICLES – TOP SCOTLAND GOALSCORERS —

#	NAME	CAREER	CAPS	GOALS
1	Kenny Dalglish	1971–1986	102	30
=	Denis Law	1958–1974	55	30
3	Hughie Gallacher	1924–1935	20	24
4	Lawrie Reilly	1948–1957	38	22
5	Ally McCoist	1986–1998	61	19
6	Robert Hamilton	1899–1911	11	15
7	Mo Johnston	1984–1991	38	14
8	Andy Wilson	1920–1923	12	13
=	Robert McColl	1896–1908	13	13
10	Alan Gilzean	1963–1971	22	12
=	Billy Steel	1947–1953	30	12
=	John Collins	1988–1999	58	12

Scottish International born this day – 5 November
Robert Buchanan (1860)

— SGIAN DUBH QUOTE —

Davie Hay still has a fresh pair of legs up his sleeve.

John Greig (44 caps)

Scottish International born this day – 6 November
John Walker (1884)

Scottish Internationals born this day – 7 November
Alexander Higgins (1863); Cornelius (Neil) Dougall (1921)

— SALTIRE SEMINAR —

In 1891, Scotland's Matt McQueen made journalists watching the match against Wales jump when his clearance smashed across the press desk, scattering the hacks' equipment over a wide area. Another effort by McQueen took off a reporter's hat, although it was said that, if the ball's trajectory had been six inches lower, it would have decapitated the young man.

— SGIAN DUBH QUOTE —

It was one of those goals that's invariably a goal.

Denis Law (55 caps)

Scottish International born this day – 8 November
James Anderson (Jimmy) Davidson (1925)

Scottish International born this day – 9 November
William Groves (1869)

— SALTIRE SEMINAR —

In the 10 years from May 1977, the Scotland international team was under the control of four different managers, not one of whom had won a full international cap as a player.

Scottish International born this day – 10 November
Robert Sharp (Bobby) Robinson (1950)

Scottish International born this day – 11 November
Neil Hamilton Dewar (1908)

Scottish Internationals born this day – 12 November
Thomas Alexander Jackson (1878); Matthew Armstrong (1911)

— SALTIRE SEMINAR —

Five Aberdeen players, Jim Leighton, Doug Rougvie, Alex McLeish, Gordon Strachan and Peter Weir, played against Northern Ireland in December 1983, while a sixth, Mark McGhee, came on as substitute.

Scottish International born this day – 13 November
Graeme Stuart Murty (1974)

Scottish Internationals born this day – 15 November
Andrew Best (Andy) Weir (1937); Ronald (Ron) Yeats (1937);
John (Jack) McGrory (1941); Joseph (Joe) Jordan (1951);
Neil Simpson (1961); Andrew David (Andy) Gray (1977)

— CALEDONIAN CHRONICLES —

Scotland usually play their home games at Hampden Park (current capacity 52,103) in Glasgow. Some matches, friendlies in particular, are occasionally played on other grounds, often Hibernian's Easter Road or Pittodrie Stadium, home of Aberdeen.

Scotland are one of a minority of UEFA members who schedule most of their matches in a city (Glasgow) that isn't the nation's capital (Edinburgh).

On some occasions competitive qualifying matches have been played at Celtic Park, Ibrox Stadium, Pittodrie and Rugby Park. All these venues hosted matches in the 1998 FIFA World Cup qualifying competition, as Hampden was having its new South Stand built. Scotland played Euro 2000 qualifiers at Celtic Park, Ibrox, Tynecastle Stadium and Pittodrie. Scotland played the Faroe Islands in their first Euro 2008 qualifier at Celtic Park, as Hampden was being used for a Robbie Williams concert.

Scottish International born this day – 14 November
David Craig (Dave) Mackay (1934); David Bruce (Dave) Smith (1943)

— SGIAN DUBH QUOTE —

As I've said before and I've said in the past...

Kenny Dalglish (102 caps)

Scottish Internationals born this day – 16 November
Peter McCloy (1946); Gary Andrew Naysmith (1979)

— SALTIRE SEMINAR —

When Scotland played Norway on 25 October 1978, the first game after Jock Stein's return as manager, the 11 Scottish players were all with English clubs.

Scottish International born this day – 17 November
John Ainslie Johnstone (1902)

— CALEDONIAN CHRONICLES —

FIFA ranking

Scotland's highest ever FIFA ranking was 14th (May 2007)

Scotland's lowest ever FIFA ranking was 88th (March 2005)

Current Top-30 FIFA ranking

20 Poland 941 UEFA
21 Uruguay 949 CONMEBOL
22 Turkey 915 UEFA
23 Scotland 913 UEFA
24 Russia 909 UEFA
25 Bosnia and Herzegovina 905 UEFA

Current FIFA zonal top-20 ranking for UEFA members only:

(Pts Jul 07)

1 Italy 1368	11 Greece 978
2 France 1357	12 Serbia 973
3 Germany 1311	13 Ukraine 973
4 Netherlands 1195	14 Sweden 918
5 Croatia 1192	15 Poland 912
6 Portugal 1146	16 Scotland 895
7 Spain 1144	17 Russia 879
8 Czech Republic 1117	18 Turkey 876
9 England 1097	19 Denmark 856
10 Romania 1068	20 Bosnia-Herzegovina 847

Scottish International born this day – 18 November
Mark Bell (1881)

— SGIAN DUBH QUOTE —

Their two wide men, who are basically wingers ...

Pat Nevin (28 caps)

Scottish International born this day – 19 November
James McLaren (1860)

— NON-PLAYING STAFF —

Scottish Football Association President: John McBeth
Manager: Alex McLeish
Assistant Managers: Andy Watson and Roy Aitkin
Under-21 Manager: Archie Knox
Under-19 Manager: Archie Gemmill
Coach: Tommy Wilton
Goalkeeping Coach: Jim Stewart
Physio: Michael McBride
Physio: Philip Yeates
Team Doctor: Dr John MacLean
Medical Officer: Professor Stewart Hillis
Player Liaison: Richard Simpson
Masseur: Mark Stoll

Scottish Internationals born this day – 20 November
William (Willie) Miller (1924); James (Jimmy) Millar (1934);
Jamie Smith (1980)

— SGIAN DUBH QUOTE —

He might play better if he shaves that beard.

Charlie Nicholas (20 caps) (on Steven Pressley)

Scottish Internationals born this day – 21 November
David Millar (Davie) Duncan (1921);
Thomas Brooks (Tommy) Craig (1950)

Scottish Internationals born this day – 22 November
William (Willie) Fernie (1928); Alexander Silcock (Alex) Scott (1936);
Francis (Frank) McAvennie (1959)

Scottish Internationals born this day – 23 November
James Tulips (Jimmy) Loggia (Logie) (1919); John Murdoch (Johnny)
MacLeod (1938); Kevin William Gallacher (1966)

— BERSERKER BIOG – HUGH KILPATRICK 'HUGHIE' GALLACHER —

Hughie was a member of the glorious Wembley Wizards side that defeated England 5–1 in 1928. He was born on 2 February 1903 in Bellshill, North Lanarkshire, and was a bright light of Scottish football in the 1920s and 30s.

This compact forward was a brilliant goalscorer and, although diminutive in stature, he was strong and brimming with instinctive skill.

The ability he demonstrated on the pitch was, at times, put in the shadow by his apparent bombastic and questionable attitude that was known to result in negative responses and repercussions both on and off the field.

Gallacher first pulled on the Scottish shirt on 1 March 1924, at Celtic

Park, Glasgow, v Northern Ireland. In all, he played 19 times for Scotland over more than 11 years, scoring a staggering 22 goals, a scoring rate of more than a goal a game that few have bettered.

During 1920 Hughie signed his first professional terms with Queen of the South, but in less than a year he left the Dumfries club for Airdrieonians. Remarkably, in four seasons Gallacher inspired the little Lanarkshire side to three Scottish League runners-up positions and a Scottish Cup.

In 1925, Newcastle United brought Hughie to England, although Airdrie fans found this hard to take, organising demonstrations against his move. Netting 23 times in 19 outings, Gallacher had an immediate impact on the Magpies and finished his first season as captain of the club.

The following term Hughie's motivational leadership ability was crucial in Newcastle's triumph in the League Championship; the Geordies had not been supreme in England since 1909.

Gallacher departed Tyneside in 1930, and signed for Chelsea. He had a five-season £10,000 contract (which, for the time, was of Beckhamesque proportions). Hughie finished his career with one-year stops at Derby County, Notts County, Grimsby Town and Gateshead.

Capable of fits of almost uncontrollable anger but also insightful and intelligent leadership, Gallacher was a controversial character and a player of huge talent. He hung up his boots with 387 goals to his credit from 541 Scottish and English League games.

The end of his life was tragic; on 11 June 1957 he committed suicide on a railway line in Gateshead.

— SGIAN DUBH QUOTE —

This game could go either way. Or it could be a draw.

Peter Lorimer (21 caps)

— SALTIRE SEMINAR —

On 14 October 1944, Scotland first wore numbered shirts for the game against England. Earlier that year, a proposal to introduce numbers had been defeated by the casting vote of the chairman. 'Numbers are all right,' he said, 'for horses and greyhounds, but not for humans.' A tad nuts from today's perspective, where players look like billboards, but you can see his point.

Scottish Internationals born this day – 24 November
Henry James Hall Marshall (1872); Robert Sime (Roy) Aitken (1958);
Thomas (Tommy) Boyd (1965)

— SGIAN DUBH QUOTE —

The main thing in a Cup tie is to get through.
Walter Smith (former Scotland manager)

Scottish Internationals born this day – 25 November
Hugh Auld Morton (1902); Alan Roderick Rough (1951);
James (Jim) Brett (1959)

— CALEDONIAN CHRONICLES —

World Cup record

Scotland have appeared in eight World Cup Finals, five times in successive tournaments from 1974 to 1990. However, the side has never played beyond the first round; goal difference denied them progression to the second round on three occasions: Brazil edged them out in 1974; in 1978 it was the Netherlands that bettered them, and, in 1982, USSR went through. Although involved in eight finals tournaments, Scotland have qualified nine times; the Scottish Football Association turned down an offer to participate in 1950 as it was thought that the team should only go to Uruguay as British champions. As it was, England were champions that year and had made it known that they wanted no part in the 'so-called' World Cup, probably considering they had won it by victory in the British Championship.

Year	Result	Matches	Wins	Draws	Losses	Goals Scored	Goals Against
1930/34/38	*Did not enter*						
1950	Withdrew						
1954	Round 1	2	0	0	2	0	8
1958	Round 1	3	0	1	2	4	6
1962/66/70	*Did not qualify*						
1974	Round 1	3	1	2	0	3	1
1978	Round 1	3	1	1	1	5	6
1982	Round 1	3	1	1	1	8	8
1986	Round 1	3	0	1	2	1	3
1990	Round 1	3	1	0	2	2	3
1994	*Did not qualify*						
1998	Round 1	3	0	1	2	2	6
2002/06	*Did not qualify*						
Total		23	4	7	12	25	41

Scottish International born this day – 26 November
William Semple (1861)

— SGIAN DUBH QUOTE —

We're down to the bare knuckles.

George Graham (12 caps)

Scottish Internationals born this day – 27 November
William Wightman Beveridge (1858); William Gillespie Boyd (1905)

— BERSERKER BIOG – JOHN ANGUS PAUL COLLINS —

Born on 31 January 1968 in Galashiels, as a youngster John played both rugby and soccer before focusing on football. As a youth, between 1980 and 1984, Collins played for Hutchison Vale and then signed professional forms with Hibernian.

In 1990, a £1m transfer took John to Celtic, the Bhoys' first seven-figure fee. Usually playing on the left side of midfield, he scored 47 goals in 217 games and was considered unlucky to have played for Celtic in a relatively unsuccessful era in the club's history; a 1995 Scottish Cup winners medal was his only memento of his time at Celtic Park.

In the summer of 1996, John moved to AS Monaco on a free transfer under the Bosman ruling. At the Stade Louis II, John won a French Championship medal in 1997 and reached the semi-final of the 1998 UEFA Champions League, beating Manchester United in the last eight. In 1998 Collins joined Everton, before concluding his playing days at Craven Cottage.

John made his international debut at the Malaz Stadium Riyad, in front of 20,000 passionate Arab supporters v Saudi Arabia, on 17 February 1988. The game ended in a 2–2 draw, Collins netting his country's second four minutes into the second half. In all, John scored 12 goals in 58 games in the blue of his nation and was part of the Scotland squads for both the Euro '96 and the 1998 World Cup tournaments. He scored in the opening match of that World Cup, converting a penalty against Brazil. In November 1999, following the aggregate defeat by England in the play-off for Euro 2000, Collins retired from international football after more than a dozen years and finished his playing career completely in the summer of 2003.

John obtained coaching qualifications, including his pro licence. He has maintained contacts with his former clubs and pleasingly was responsible for introducing Collins John to Fulham in 2004.

John became manager of Hibernian on 31 October 2006. His first victory as a manager came on 8 November 2006, a satisfying local derby 1–0 win against Hearts.

Collins took Hibs to their first trophy in 16 years when they beat Kilmarnock 5–1 in the Scottish League Cup Final on 18 March 2007.

But there were to be serious difficulties between Collins and his players later that same season, and he was criticised for constantly changing the side and formation.

Scottish Internationals born this day – 28 November
Frank Haffey (1938); Gavin Rae (1977)

— SGIAN DUBH QUOTE —

My bum has been through every temperature known to man.
Gordon Strachan (50 caps) (on heat treatment and ice-packs, 1993)

Scottish Internationals born this day – 29 November
John Browning (1888); John (Jock) Shaw (1912);
Hugh Robertson (1939)

Scottish Internationals born this day – 30 November
George Graham (1944); Andrew Mullen (Andy) Gray (1955);
Brian McAllister (1970); Robert Keith (Robbie) Stockdale (1979)

— SALTIRE SEMINAR —

One of the 149,000 people that turned up for the 1937 Scotland v England match at Hampden Park after the game told Bob McPhail, 'I didn't have room to move. I was almost squeezed to death.'

McPhail replied, 'You should have been where I was, I had plenty of room.' McPhail netted twice late on to give Scotland their win.

Scottish Internationals born this day – 1 December
Stephen (Steve) Nicol (1961); Simon Thomas Donnelly (1974)

Scottish International born this day – 2 December
Christopher (Chris) Burke (1983)

— SGIAN DUBH QUOTE —

The referee has a reputation for trying to make a name for himself.

Graeme Souness (54 caps)

Scottish International born this day – 3 December
Robert (Bobby) Dougan (1926);
Thomas Valley (Tosh) McKinlay (1964)

Scottish International born this day – 4 December
Alexander Donaldson (1890)

Scottish International born this day – 5 December
Arthur Duncan (1947)

Scottish International born this day – 6 December
Gordon Scott Durie (1965)

— SALTIRE SEMINAR —

Eddie Gray missed a game with Switzerland in April 1976, and so was denied the opportunity to play in the same Scotland side as his brother Frank. The Scotland team did include two Grays, Frank and Andy, but they were not related.

Scottish Internationals born this day – 7 December
George Hamilton (1917); Hugh Brown (1921);
John Francombe (Ian) Ure (1939);
Desmond George (Des) Bremner (1952);
Edward Colin James (Colin) Hendry (1965)

Scottish Internationals born this day – 8 December
John Anderson (1929); Ralph Laidlaw Brand (1936);
Douglas Michael (Doug) Fraser (1941);
Robert Munro (Bobby) McKean (1952);
Brian John McClair (1963)

— SALTIRE SEMINAR —

When Scotland qualified for the 1978 World Cup in Argentina (England had failed to qualify), manager Ally MacLeod told the world that his side was capable of winning the championship. This optimism was mirrored by comedian Andy Cameron whose jaunty refrain made the record charts shortly before Scotland left for South America.

> We're on the march wi' Ally's Army,
> We're going tae the Argentine,
> And we'll really shake them up,
> When we win the World Cup,
>
> 'Cos Scotland is the greatest football team.

> We're representing Britain,
> And we're gaunny do or die,
> England cannae dae it,
> 'Cos they didnae qualify!

> We're on the march wi' Ally's Army,
> We're going tae the Argentine,
> And we'll really shake them up,
> When we win the World Cup,
> 'Cos Scotland is the greatest football team.

Many of Scotland's Tartan Army of football fans caught the optimism prompted by Ally and Andy, but it all ended in tears when Scotland failed to get out of their first-round group and the lasting image of Scotland's participation was of MacLeod, head buried in his hands, a picture of despair.

Scottish International born this day – 9 December
William John (Billy) Bremner (1942)

— CALEDONIAN CHRONICLES —

European Championship record

Scotland have qualified for two European Championships but have not advanced further than the first round on both occasions. At Euro 1996 their progress was restricted only by the better goal difference of the Netherlands.

Qualifying games for Euro 2008 started in 2006. Scotland's form improved as the tournament progressed, but expectations were not high, the group they were drawn in being dubbed 'the group of death'.

Year	Result	Games	Win	Draw	Lost	Goals Scored	Goals Against
1960/1964	Did not enter						
1968/1972/1976/1980/1984/1988	Did not qualify						
1992	Round 1	3	1	0	2	3	3
1996	Round 1	3	1	1	1	1	2
2000/2004	Did not qualify						
Total		6	2	1	3	4	5

— SGIAN DUBH QUOTE —

He's got two great feet. Left foot, right foot, either side.

Alan Hansen (26 caps)

— SALTIRE SEMINAR —

The Dakota carrying the Scotland party to Belgium in 1947 overshot the runway at Brussels, and the pilot had to lift the aircraft back into the air. The game was played in the Heysel Stadium, then in poor condition following its use as a German tank park. It seems the whole experience was too much for Scotland who left a defeated team.

Scottish Internationals born this day – 10 December
Andrew Wilson (1880); Michael (Mike) Haughney (1926)

Scottish Internationals born this day – 11 December
Thomas Tindal Fitchie (1881); Denis Lawson (1897)

— BERSERKER BIOG – WILLIAM 'BILLY' MCNEILL MBE —

Billy was known as Cesar to Scottish and Celtic supporters alike. He got this moniker after being associated with the actor Cesar Romero, who played the getaway driver in (the original) *Ocean's Eleven*. Bill was one of the few Celtic players to own a car at the time.

McNeill was amongst the greatest skippers ever to wear the green of Celtic. He was born on 2 March 1940 to a Roman Catholic family in Bellshill, North Lanarkshire, but has a dual Irish/Lithuanian heritage.

Billy started playing for his local junior team, Blantyre Victoria, and was picked up by Celtic in 1957. He rose to the status of club captain and won nine Scottish League Championship, seven Scottish Cup and six Scottish League Cup medals. Of course, Billy led Celtic to European Cup victory in 1967, as captain of the Lisbon Lions, and became the first British footballer to lift the European Cup in triumph.

McNeill finished his playing career in 1975; he had made over 800 appearances for Celtic, and won 29 caps, making his international debut against England at Wembley in the terrible 9–3 destruction of the Scottish side on 15 April 1961. His international career lasted over a decade and Billy captained his country eight times and scored three goals for Scotland.

Billy started his managerial career in April 1977 with Clyde, but in June of that year he moved to Aberdeen. However, he returned to his roots to manage Celtic in 1978. A half-decade reign at Celtic Park brought three League Championships, one Scottish Cup and one League Cup.

In 1983, McNeill took on the role of manager with Manchester City and during the 1986/87 season he became one of the few managers to preside over two clubs on the road to relegation in the same season. He started the season in control of Manchester City, but resigned in September 1986 and took charge of fellow strugglers Aston Villa.

However, after Villa were relegated in May 1987, concluding their season bottom of the old First Division, Billy left the club and returned to Celtic.

In his first season back in Scotland, Billy led the Bhoys to a League and Scottish Cup double, which added immeasurably to the celebrations of the club's centenary year. The 1987/88 campaign became a tale of belated goals for Celtic; in both the semi-final and final of the Cup, the Hoops scored late goals to emerge 2–1 winners. This was indicative of McNeill's 'no surrender' attitude.

Billy guided Celtic to the Scottish Cup the following season, but left the club in 1991 after four years. His second period as manager was soured by the Board's reticence to spend money on new players.

In 2003, McNeill stood as a candidate for the Scottish Senior Citizens Unity Party in the election of the Scottish Parliament, but he was unsuccessful.

Scottish International born this day – 12 December
John Davidson Hewie (1928)

Scottish Internationals born this day – 13 December
George Law (1885); Eoin Jess (1970)

— SALTIRE SEMINAR —

Joe Craig scored a goal with his first touch in international football. Coming on as a 76th-minute substitute v Sweden at Hampden Park for Kenny Burns on 27 April 1977, Craig scored with his head after being on the field for less than three minutes. With earlier goals by Kenny Dalglish (55 mins) and Asa Hartford (30 mins), Scotland won the game 3–1.

Scottish Internationals born this day – 14 December
John Paterson (1896); Peter Patrick Lorimer (1946);
Allan Johnston (1973)

Scottish International born this day – 15 December
David Thomson (Dave) Robb (1947)

— SGIAN DUBH QUOTE —

Craig Bellamy has literally been on fire.

Ally McCoist (61 caps)

Scottish Internationals born this day – 16 December
William Barbour Agnew (1879); Thomas (Tommy) Burns (1956);
Scott Booth (1971); Gareth John Williams (1981)

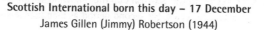

> **Scottish International born this day – 17 December**
> James Gillen (Jimmy) Robertson (1944)

— SGIAN DUBH QUOTE —

Every time they attacked we were memorised by them.

Charlie Nicholas (20 caps)

> **Scottish Internationals born this day – 18 December**
> John Alexander Lambie (1868); William (Willie) Toner (1929)

> **Scottish International born this day – 19 December**
> William (Willie) Johnston (1946)

— SALTIRE SEMINAR —

On 15 April 1939, conditions were so poor at Hampden that both England and Scotland were obliged to change their shirts at half-time (such was the mud that the 22 players could not be distinguished one from another). England borrowed a set from Queen's Park.

> **Scottish International born this day – 20 December**
> James (Jim) Herriott (1939)

> **Scottish International born this day – 21 December**
> Archibald Gray (1883)

— BERSERKER BIOG – JOHN GREIG MBE —

Born 11 September 1942 in Edinburgh, in his boyhood Greig was devoted to his local club Heart of Midlothian, but his whole playing career was played out at Ibrox Park.

A powerful and focused defender, John played 857 games for Rangers (he achieved a club record of 496 League appearances) and won three domestic trebles in the process. Greig was Rangers' skipper when the club won the European Cup Winners Cup in 1972, defeating Dynamo Moscow 3–2 in Barcelona.

After making his debut for Scotland on 11 April 1964 in front of 133,245 fans at Hampden Park, who cheered the home side to a 1–0 victory over the English, John had a seven-year international career during which he earned 44 caps and acted as Scotland's captain 15 times.

Perhaps Greig's most memorable moment in a Scottish shirt was his late winner on 9 November 1965 in Scotland's 1–0 victory against Italy at Hampden Park.

John was manager of Rangers from 1978 to 1983 – oddly, he replaced and was replaced by Jock Wallace. Greig's reign at Ibrox was not a golden one and the low attendances at the end of his tenure were something of an indictment. But he left a strong legacy, having signed the man who would become Rangers' greatest ever goalscorer – Ally McCoist from Sunderland.

In 1999 John was voted 'The Greatest Ever Ranger' by the club's fans and, in 2003, he joined the Rangers Board of Directors, so extending his long association with the club.

Greig has been immortalised by a statue erected outside Ibrox. It also acts as a memorial for and depicts the tragic events that happened during the Ibrox Stadium Disaster of 1971 when 66 people lost their lives.

Scottish International born this day – 22 December
Bryan James Gunn (1963)

Scottish International born this day – 23 December
Kenneth (Kenny) Miller (1979)

— SALTIRE SEMINAR —

'Six foot two, eyes of blue, Big Jim Holton's after you' was one of the Scottish fans' favourite refrains of the 1974 World Cup. It alludes to the steely-eyed and uncompromising centre-half Jim Holton. Willie Ormond, the Scottish manager at the time, once said of Jim that he had no injuries in training as he was playing everybody on Holton's side.

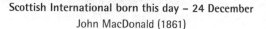

Scottish International born this day – 24 December
John MacDonald (1861)

— SGIAN DUBH QUOTE —

I watched the game, and I saw an awful lot of it.

Andy Gray (20 caps)

Scottish International born this day – 25 December
Gary McAllister (1964)

Scottish International born this day – 26 December
Stephen (Steve) Chalmers (1936)

— SALTIRE SEMINAR —

Motherwell player Ben Ellis turned out for Scotland on the 1939 North American tour; however, he had previously received six Welsh caps in the 1930s.

Scottish Internationals born this day – 27 December
John McPhail (1923); Duncan Ferguson (1971)

Scottish International born this day – 28 December
Francis (Frank) McLintock (1939)

Scottish International born this day – 29 December
Robert (Bobby) Shearer (1931)

Scottish Internationals born this day – 30 December
William (Billy) Hughes (1948); Charles (Charlie) Nicholas (1961);
Paul Robert Bernard (1972)

— SGIAN DUBH QUOTE —

*He's captain of Rangers, and that's one of the reasons
he's captain.*

Walter Smith (former Scotland manager)

Scottish Internationals born this day – 31 December
William Pullar James (Sandy) Jardine (1948); Craig Gordon (1982)

— BERSERKER BIOG – ALEXANDER WILSON JAMES —

Although James had a phenomenal club career, he won just eight caps for Scotland over seven years. He made his international debut against Wales on 31 October 1925 in his country's 0–3 win at Ninian Park, Cardiff. But the highlight of his time with Scotland was probably in 1928 during his second international game when he was one of the Wembley Wizards. He scored twice (both Scotland's goals in the second half).

James was born on 14 September 1901 in Mossend, Lanarkshire. An inside-forward, supporting the main strikers, he was renowned for the quality of his passing and fantastic ball control.

Alex suffered with rheumatism, and donned extra baggy shorts (in a time when baggy shorts were the only option) to hide the long johns he wore to keep warm; his name was to become synonymous with these voluminous bottoms.

After beginning his career with local youth-club sides, in 1922 James signed for Raith Rovers and spent three seasons at Starks Park, notching up over 100 League appearances, before joining Preston North End in 1925. He spent four years with the Second Division side, netting 55 times in 157 outings for the Lilywhites. However, near the end of his stay at Deepdale, he got involved with a series of disputes with management. It appeared wages were part of the problem. At the time the Football League operated a maximum wage of £8 a week, but other clubs found ways to 'compensate' for this with their bigger stars. At the same time Preston refused to release James for international matches.

James left Preston in 1929 to join Herbert Chapman's Arsenal. The fee was £8,750, a huge amount of money at the time. He made his debut for the Gunners on 31 August 1928 against Leeds United. In order to get around wage rules, James was found a job at Selfridges, where he was paid £250 a year as a 'sports demonstrator'.

Although Alex's initial season at Highbury was unimpressive, he eventually settled into the side and became part of the Arsenal team that dominated English football in 1930s. He was Chapman's midfield maestro and became one of the club's greatest ever players. As an Arsenal player, he has been compared to Dennis Bergkamp, but this does not do him justice. While the Dutchman had a huge depth of skill in certain areas, James had a width of talent that was a dimension beyond Bergkamp's well-disciplined approach.

The deep supportive role played by James meant that he scored relatively few goals, just 27 in 261 games, but he made many dozens more. His passing and vision fed David Jack, Cliff Bastin, Ted Drake and Jack Lambert and together they won the First Division Championship four times in five seasons (1931, 1933, 1934 and 1935), and two FA Cups; Alex scored the first goal of the 1930 final (the Gunners' first major trophy), and skippered Arsenal to their 1936 victory over Sheffield United. James missed the 1932 final against Newcastle United and Arsenal lost 2–1 after a controversial goal from the Magpies' Jack Allen, but many saw the absence of James as the reason for the Gunners losing out.

James finished his playing career in 1937. He served in the Royal Artillery during World War II, after which he became a journalist. In 1949, Alex was asked to return to Highbury as coach to the youth side.

James died suddenly from cancer on 1 June 1953 at the tragically young age of 51.

In 2005 Alex was inducted into the English Football Hall of Fame in recognition of his contribution to the game.

James was given an odd slice of flattery when he was mentioned in the song 'With Her Head Tucked Underneath Her Arm', a popular monologue by Stanley Holloway first penned in 1926 but which remained well known into the 1960s.

— SALTIRE SEMINAR —

When they first started playing internationals, Ireland wore light-blue shirts, but, if the light was poor on the days when they played Scotland, it was often difficult to tell which of the players were Scottish and which were Irish.

— THE IMMORTAL SHANKS —

Bill Shankly only played for Scotland five times, but he is one of the greatest names in football and certainly amongst the most influential personalities to come out of the Scottish game. He had a great feeling for language, and probably summed up the nature of the sport and the characters that are part of it better than anyone.

After Tommy Lawrence (Liverpool and Scotland) had let in a fluke goal between his legs: 'Sorry, boss, I should have kept my legs together,' said Lawrence.

'No, Tommy, your mother should have kept her legs together!' replied Bill.

Adidas wanted to present Shanks with a Golden Boot for services to football. Bob Paisley took the call and told him, 'They want to know what shoe size you take.'

Shanks replied, 'If it's gold, tell them I'm a 28.'

I don't believe everything Bill tells me about his players. If they were that good, they'd not only have won the European Cup but the Ryder Cup, the Boat Race and even the Grand National!

Jock Stein (on Bill Shankly)

Shanks's Wisdom

Football is a simple game based on the giving and taking of passes, of controlling the ball and of making yourself available to receive a pass. It is terribly simple.

If you are first you are first. If you are second you are nothing.

I don't think I was in a bath until I was 15 years old. I used to use a tub to wash myself. But out of poverty with a lot of people living in the same house, you get humour

What can you do, playing against 11 goalposts?

After a 0–0 draw

The best side drew.

My life is my work. My work is my life.

If a player is not interfering with play or seeking to gain an advantage, then he should be.

He's not just the best centre-forward in the British Isles, but the only one.

Bill talking about Brian Clough

He's worse than the rain in Manchester. At least God stops the rain in Manchester occasionally.

Again about Cloughie

A football team is like a piano. You need eight men to carry it and three who can play the damn thing.

I was only in the game for the love of football – and I wanted to bring back happiness to the people.

Son, you'll do well here as long as you remember two things. Don't over-eat and don't lose your accent.

Instructions to Ian St John on the day he signed for Liverpool

Jock, do you want your share of the gate money or shall we just return the empties?

To Jock Stein after the 1966 Cup Winners Cup tie with Celtic at Anfield

He's got the heart of a caraway seed.

About a player he had just sold

A lot of football success is in the mind. You must believe you are the best and then make sure that you are.

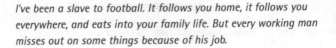
I've been a slave to football. It follows you home, it follows you everywhere, and eats into your family life. But every working man misses out on some things because of his job.

The trouble with referees is that they know the rules, but they do not know the game.

Just tell them I completely disagree with everything they say.
Instructing an interpreter regarding excited Italian journalists

I told this player, 'Listen, son, you haven't broken your leg. It's all in the mind.'

We absolutely annihilated England. It was a massacre. We beat them 5–4.
Remembering a wartime England v Scotland match

The problem with you, son, is that all your brains are in your head.

Someone said, 'Football is more important than life and death to you,' and I said, 'Listen, it's more important than that.'

I'm a people's man – only the people matter.

I was the best manager in Britain because I was never devious or cheated anyone. I'd break my wife's legs if I played against her, but I'd never cheat her.

It's a 90-minute game for sure. In fact, I used to train for a 190-minute game so that when the whistle blew at the end of the match I could have played another 90 minutes.

The socialism I believe in is everybody working for the same goal and everybody having a share in the rewards. That's how I see football, that's how I see life.

— BIBLIOGRAPHY —

Butler, B. (1987) *The Football League 1888–1988. The Official Illustrated History*, Queen Ann Press

Cairney, J. (1998) *A Scottish Football Hall of Fame*, Mainstream

Cook, C. and Stevenson, J. (1988) *Modern British History*, Longman

Fabian, A. H. and Green, G. (eds) (1961) *Associated Football*, London: Caxton

Farror, M. and Lamming, D. (1972) *A Century of English International Football 1872–1972*, London: Hale

Hayes, D. (2006) *Scotland! Scotland!* Mercat Press

Hugman, B. (1998) *The PFA Premier & Football League Players Records 1946–2006*, Queen Anne Press

Hutchinson, J. (1982) *The Football Industry*, R. Drew

Inglis, S. (1987) *The Football Grounds of Great Britain*, Willow

James, B. (1970) *England v Scotland*, Sportsmans Book Club

Johnston, F. (ed.) (1934) *The Football Encyclopedia*, Associated Sporting Press

Joyce, N. (2004) *Football League Players' Records 1888 to 1939*, Soccer Data

Keir, R. (2001) *Scotland; The Complete International Football Record*, Breedon Books

McAvennie, F. (2003) *Scoring: An Expert's Guide*, Canongate

Oliver, G. (1995) *World Soccer* (2nd Ed), Guinness

Potter, D. (2004) *Wizards and Bravehearts*, Tempus

Leatherdale, C. (1994) *Scotland: Quest for the World Cup – A Complete Record, 1950–94*, Desert Island

Ross, A. and Robinson, P (eds) *Scotland 1872–1960*, Soccer Book Publishing

Thompson, P. and Hale, S. (2004) *Shankly*, Tempus

Ward, A. (1987) *Scotland: The Team*, Breedon Books

Wall, F. (1935) *Fifty Years of Football*, London: Cassel & Co.

Walvin, J. (1975) *The People's Game. A Social History of British Football*, Newton Abbot: A. Lane

Publications

Athletic News

Daily Mail

Daily Mirror

Daily News and Leader

Evening Post

The Field

Football Chat

Football News

Football Players' Magazine

Football Sun

Saturday Night and Football Sun

Soccer History

Sporting Chronicle

Sunday Pictorial

The Daily Record Newspaper 1895–2000

The Footballer

The Glasgow Herald Newspaper 1872–2000

The Sportsman

Sports Times

The Times

Websites

http://www.rsssf.com/tabless/scot-intres.html

http://www.scottishfa.co.uk/index.cfm?curpageid=148

— GLOSSARY —

Sgian Dubh Ceremonial dagger (Gaelic sgian) worn as part of the modern Scottish Highland dress.

Dead riddie Blush with embarrassment.

Saltire St Andrew's Cross – a heraldic symbol in the form of a diagonal cross or letter X. Legend relates it to a diagonal cross that St Andrew is said to have been martyred on. It forms the national flag of Scotland (and Jamaica).

Berserker Legendary Scottish warriors.

Barry (Bar-ee) Splendid, good, wonderful.

Rammy A fight, conflict – 'There wis a right rammy efter ra gemm.'

Brae Hill.